The
Satisfied
Heart

The Satisfied Heart

31 Days of Experiencing God's Love

Ruth Myers

WATERBROOK
PRESS

THE SATISFIED HEART: *31 Days of Experiencing God's Love*
PUBLISHED BY WATERBROOK PRESS
12265 Oracle Boulevard, Suite 200
Colorado Springs, Colorado 80921
A division of Random House, Inc.

Scriptures given in this book include direct quotations, as well as the author's adapted and combined quotations, from the following translations and paraphrases:

Amplified — *The Amplified Bible,* copyright 1965, Zondervan Publishing House.

Berkeley — *The Berkeley Version in Modern English,* copyright New Testament 1945, Old Testament 1959, Zondervan Publishing House.

KJV — *King James Version.*

Moffatt — *The Bible: A New Translation* by James Moffatt, copyright 1950, 1952, 1953, 1954, James Moffatt.

NASB — *New American Standard Bible,* copyright The Lockman Foundation, 1960, 1962, 1963, 1968, 1971, 1973, 1975, 1977.

NCV — *The New Century Version,* copyright 1987, 1988, 1991 by Word Publishing.

NEB — *The New English Bible,* copyright 1961, 1970, the Delegates of the Oxford University Press and the Syndics of the Cambridge University Press.

NIV — *The Holy Bible: New International Version,* copyright 1985 by the Zondervan Corporation.

NKJV — *The New King James Version,* copyright 1979, 1980, 1982, Thomas Nelson, Inc., Publishers.

NLT — *The Holy Bible: New Living Translation,* copyright 1996, Tyndale House Publishers, Inc.

NRSV — *The New Revised Standard Version of the Bible,* copyright 1989 by the Division of Christian Education of the National Council of the Churches of Christ in the USA.

Phillips — *The New Testament in Modern English,* J. B. Phillips, copyright J. B. Phillips, 1958, 1960, 1972, Macmillan Publishing Company.

RSV — *Revised Standard Version Bible,* copyright 1946, 1952, 1971, the Division of Christian Education of the National Council of the Churches of Christ in the USA.

TEV — *Good News Bible: Today's English Version,* copyright 1976, American Bible Society.

TLB — *The Living Bible,* copyright 1971, Tyndale House Publishers.

Wuest — *The New Testament: An Expanded Translation,* Kenneth S. Wuest, copyright 1961, Wm. B. Eerdmans Publishing Company.

All used by permission, all rights reserved.

All *italics* in Scripture quotations are the author's.

10 Digit ISBN 1-57856-278-3
13 Digit ISBN 978-1-57856-278-7

Printed in the United States of America
2007

10 9 8 7

Contents

As You Begin

My prayer for you as you follow these daily devotions is that the Lord will lead you into a rich experience of His love that will keep growing as the days and months and years go by.

To help it grow, I encourage you to explore the Scriptures listed at the end of each daily section. Ask yourself, "Which of these verses catches my attention most?" At the bottom of the page or in a notebook, you may want to write down this verse or the portion of it that you especially like.

The following passage has inspired me for many years to pursue a deeper experience of God. I pray it will do the same for you.

If you accept my words
and store up my commands within you,
turning your ear to wisdom
and applying your heart to understanding,

and if you call out for insight
and cry aloud for understanding,
and if you look for it as for silver
and search for it as for hidden treasure,
then you will understand the fear of the LORD
and find the knowledge of God.

(PROVERBS 2:1-5, NIV)

Dear Lord, I ask You to be the One speaking through this book. Reveal Yourself, minister to the reader's heart, quicken his or her love for You—and do anything else You want to do through these pages.

In Jesus' name.

First Love

When I was ten, God (and my mother) used a famous verse about His love to give me my first conscious experience of it.

Four years earlier I had gone forward in an evangelistic meeting. The pastor had talked with me about the gospel and I prayed. Soon I was baptized and became a church member. But later on, all I could remember was my baptism. I knew about the cross of Christ and about His resurrection, but I remembered no personal contact with God. And I didn't know where I would go if I died. This worried me. So whenever our pastor began preaching on hell, I'd slip out of the service, pretending I needed to go to the rest room.

One night my mother, sensing that something was troubling me, asked me about it. I didn't really want to tell her about the struggle in my heart, for she thought I was a real Christian. But I admitted my fear concerning my eternal destiny.

In reply Mother did something so simple. She quoted a verse I'd known for as long as I could remember. But as she spoke, the truth dawned in my heart and I believed: "God so *loved* the world, that he gave his only begotten Son, that whosoever believeth in him should not perish, but have everlasting life." That night I believed in Christ as *my* Savior, and my fear and guilt rolled away. That night, for the first time I remember, I felt God's love. All this happened in an instant as Mother quoted John 3:16 (KJV). When she finished, I bowed my head and thanked the Lord that He had given me eternal life.

"I'LL DO ANYTHING"

When I entered my teenage years, I didn't know any Christian young people who, as far as I could tell, were really living the Christian life. I had one friend a few years older who loved the Lord, but she seemed rather old-maidish and I didn't want to be like her. So I decided I wouldn't follow the Lord closely.

Behind this decision were wrong ideas about God. I didn't believe He wanted what was best for me. I was afraid that if I gave Him the controls, He would make me do things I didn't want to do and I'd miss the best in life. In this time of rebellion I tried everything I dared, though sometimes the Holy Spirit blocked me. And I became more and more miserable.

Finally at age sixteen I agreed to attend a Christian conference. There I saw young people on fire for the Lord, and I received a lot of solid Bible teaching. One night I went outside under the trees and prayed, "Lord, I'll do *anything* You want me to—even be a missionary," which was the very worst thing I could think of.

During the next few years God began to deepen my appreciation for His love through "The Love of God," a song made famous by George Beverly Shea. This song describes God's love as "greater far than tongue or pen can ever tell." If the skies were a scroll and the oceans filled with ink, the song says, and if every stalk on earth were a writing quill, we still could never write in full this love God has for us. The skies could not contain it. The oceans of ink would run dry.

Singing those words I truly *felt* the love of God. I knew that He understands, that He cares, that He is compassionate. I needed this knowledge then, and I still need it every day. But I had not yet learned to let my roots go down deep into His love so that it was a constant influence in my life. I felt His love primarily when I was singing about it with others, but not when I was alone or when things went wrong.

As the Lord worked within me, my desires for the future gradually made a U-turn. I found I wanted to become a missionary after all, and I began preparing for this. A favorite verse became Psalm 84:11: "No good thing will He withhold from those who walk uprightly" (NKJV). As I followed God, I was discovering He knew better than I did how to satisfy me. Life was getting better, though not necessarily easier.

MAJOR PURSUIT

After I was graduated from high school, I set out for Northwestern Bible School and College in Minneapolis. There the Lord did more new things in my heart. I'd been having daily devotions since I was sixteen. Often it was the last thing I did at night, and I could hardly hold my eyes open. Nevertheless, I congratulated myself for being such a good Christian.

Then the Lord began speaking: "Ruth, that's not the point at all. I want you to come to My Word because you want to know Me." The lesson was reinforced for me by the hymn "Break Thou the Bread of Life" in the lines that say,

"Beyond the sacred page I seek *thee,* Lord; my spirit pants *for thee,* O Living Word." I still wanted Him to teach me the principles I should know from the Bible, but I began going to Him more often with the prayer, "Lord, most of all I want to know You." Since that request is in line with God's will for His children, He answered it just as He promised in 1 John 5:14-15.

There was one fellow in school who, more than anyone else, seemed set upon knowing the Lord, and I greatly admired him. Stan had plenty of work and study responsibilities, and between those and his pursuit of the Lord, he didn't have time for dating. Being a little beyond my reach made him all the more desirable. I learned that one of Stan's favorite Scripture passages was from Philippians 3. I began to pray over it—and to cry over it, for I was learning that I had to get my heart needs met in my relationship with Jesus Christ and not anywhere else. The passage soon became a favorite of mine as well. Verses 8 and 10 in the *Amplified Bible* (condensed a bit) read,

> *I count everything as loss compared to the priceless privilege—the surpassing worth and supreme advantage—of knowing Christ Jesus my Lord.... For His sake I have lost everything and consider it all to be*

mere rubbish, in order that I may gain Christ....
[For my determined purpose is] that I may know
Him—that I may progressively become more deeply
and intimately acquainted with Him, perceiving and
recognizing and understanding [the wonders of His
Person] more strongly and more clearly.

Nothing else meant anything to Paul compared to the priceless privilege of knowing this vastly wonderful Person he had met. Back then I didn't have the Amplified version but I did have Philippians 3:10 in the King James: "That I may know him." I began to hear God say, "Ruth, this must be your major pursuit." He used circumstances to drive me to my knees and to begin praying along this line. And, as a young single woman, I discovered that the Lord could and did meet my deepest longing if I let Him be my first love.

My younger sister Mary eventually joined me at Northwestern, and we found a poem, the source of which is unknown, that we often reflected on and used in prayer:

Purge me, Lord, of my follies; an empty cup let me be,
Waiting only Thy blessing, hungry only for Thee.
Can even the Lord pour blessing into a cup that is full?
Put treasure into a locked hand, be He ever so bountiful?

Empty me, Lord, and make me hungry only for Thee.
Only Thy bread once tasted can ever satisfy me.

DESIRED AND DESIRING

Then came another crucial lesson from the Lord, a brand-new revelation for me: Not only was He compassionate and understanding, not only was He always there to tenderly care for me and love me, but He also *desired* me. He longed for fellowship with me.

Sometime later I realized how strongly this truth had impressed me as I talked with a friend in college, a tough young man just out of the navy. Doug told me one day that he'd been having trouble getting out of bed for his morning quiet time. But he had found a verse that helped him. It was in Proverbs (I soon forgot the reference because I didn't feel inclined to write it down): "How long wilt thou sleep, O sluggard? When wilt thou arise out of thy sleep?"

Well, I thought, *that's fine for Doug. But I don't want to wake up to that.* I preferred hearing the Lord speak to me through Song of Solomon 2:13-14—"Arise, my love, my fair one, and come away.… Let me see your face, let me hear your voice, for your voice is sweet, and your face is comely" (RSV). How could the Lord say that to *me?* Because in Christ I stand forgiven and cleansed, and in my innermost being

I'm beautiful with His beauty. Amazing! To think that my appearance is pleasing to God, that my voice is sweet, that He desires intimate fellowship with me! What a motivation to spend time with Him.

Later I was struck by these words from an unknown author:

My goal is God Himself,
Not peace or joy
Or even blessing,
But Himself, my God.
'Tis His to lead me there—
Not mine, but His.
At any cost, dear Lord,
By any road.

Another truth dawned on my heart during that time—a truth that revolutionized my life. I found this truth in capsule form in Colossians 3:4—"Christ…is your life." And I personalized it to say, "Christ is *my* life." As one man of God put it, "It's not only true that my life is *Christ's,* but my life is *Christ.*"

How delightful it was to learn that Christ my Savior, the Lord of love, triumphant over sin and death, is my life!

His Spirit is united with mine in a permanent union (1 Corinthians 6:17). And as I live by faith in Him, His Spirit unveils truth to me, empowers me to do His will, and pours out His love in my heart (Galatians 2:20, Philippians 2:13, Romans 5:5). What a vast difference this makes in how I view myself: I am united in the most intimate way with the Lover of my soul. I am able to enjoy His divine, self-sacrificing love and, with growing depth and constancy, to channel it to other people.

Once a year during my time at Northwestern, an elderly Southern gentleman would speak for a week in our daily chapel services. His name was Dad Byus. He wasn't particularly impressive in appearance; what I remember most were three funny little pin curls of white hair hanging down his forehead. But he radiated Christ. As he preached, he would suddenly burst out singing, "My wonderful Lord, my wonderful Lord, by angels and seraphs in heaven adored," and we would all join in. He often quoted these words: "I have seen the face of Jesus; tell me not of ought beside. I have heard the voice of Jesus, and my soul is satisfied." The Lord used this man's teaching to make me more hungry for Him.

The same year that Mary joined me at Northwestern, two identical twin brothers enrolled and were noticed by everyone. They were handsome, they dressed attractively, they were musical, and they walked closely with the Lord. And they were the same age I was. Lots of girls liked the Denler twins. Mary and I did too, but we didn't think they'd ever like us. My sister was so dogmatic about this that I said, "Mary, you can't be *that* sure about anything."

The twins didn't date anyone that first year. But the next fall Dean Denler asked me to go with him to an upcoming stage play, the big production of the school year. On the same day Gene Denler asked Mary. I found out later that Dean told his brother, "Ruth said yes, but she sure didn't look very enthusiastic." The fact was, I was shocked.

Mary and I talked about this upcoming date as we left the campus that evening, heading for home. At first our conversation was along the lines of how lucky can a girl be? Then the Lord brought to mind Psalm 73:25-26, a passage we had memorized: "Whom have I in heaven but You? And there is none upon earth that I desire besides You" (NKJV). God was reminding us that He was to be our first love. I don't think this verse means we can't or shouldn't have any other desires. Rather it's saying, "Lord, in comparison to my desire for You, I desire no one else. If ever I must choose between You and any other, I'll choose You."

Verse 26 goes on, "My flesh and my heart fail; but God is the strength of my heart and my portion forever." We both felt that going out with the Denlers would surely be a one-time event, but God would be our portion forever—all through life and all through eternity. Only one relationship is sure to be lifelong. Only one Person is for sure our permanent life partner. And He is our best life partner, worthy above all others of being our first love.

The Lord reminded me of this truth many times. I'm so grateful He did.

PLOWING TIME

It turned out to be more than one date. Within two years we were engaged: Mary to Gene, and I to Dean. The Lord (through the Navigators) sent the twins ahead of us to Taiwan to pursue ministry opportunities there.

On our way to join them a year and a half later, Mary and I spent half a day with Lila Trotman, the wife of Dawson Trotman, founder of the Navigators. Lila knew that our future husbands would often be traveling in their ministry responsibilities. "Just remember," she told us, "God will make up for every moment you're apart." Then she added, "And He won't wait to do it until you're back together again." In other words, God would make up for our loss *with Himself.*

My inner response to Lila's gracious counsel was, "Yes,

Lord, You are well able to do this, and You will—if I let You." This realization was great preparation not only for marriage but also for the time, seven years later, when God would call Dean home.

Soon it was time to cross the Pacific on a comfortable American President Lines freighter. Mary and I were so excited. To be used by the Lord in Asia had become the dream of our hearts, and now in 1952 this dream was coming true—as were our dreams of becoming Mrs. Denler.

A week after we arrived in Taiwan we had a double wedding in Taipei, then we headed to Hong Kong for our honeymoons. Afterward Mary and Gene flew off to the Philippines to serve the Lord there, and I went with Dean to southern Taiwan. Mary and I had always been close, the twins had been even closer, and most of our dating had been as couples together. So we were facing some adjustments.

Lots of them, in fact. And we had received little prior help on how to handle them. Decades later, I helped conduct many two- to three-month orientation programs to help western missionaries prepare for life in Asia. But back in 1952, new missionaries received just one bit of counsel on how to respond to all the unfamiliar ways of the Chinese culture: "Not wrong, but different." This was sound advice from a veteran missionary and dear friend, Dick Hillis, founder of Overseas Crusades. It has helped often in building relationships as well as in adjusting to other cultures. But entering another culture involves more than that.

In our new surroundings we did not yet know the language. I began to miss greatly the rich Christian fellowship I had long known. A few older missionaries were in our city, and that helped a lot. But being with them just wasn't the same as relating to loved ones and people our own age. Also, back in America I had enjoyed helping other young women grow in their faith, and I missed that as well.

Two big surprises made our adjustments even more complex: Dean and I had our children earlier than we had planned. From the first we were grateful for those precious gifts from our sovereign God. And later I was so glad that Brian was six and Doreen almost five when their father died—old enough to have memories of him, old enough for me to communicate with them, and easier to care for than if they were still babies or toddlers.

Those years in Taiwan were good in so many ways, but they were hard years. They were a time of plowing in my life, when the steel of the plow was cutting deep into my soul. I could no longer feel the love of God as easily as I had before. I would tell Him, "Lord, I don't know what's happening to me. I don't know why my emotions don't cooperate like they used to." Then I would remember Hebrews 13:8 where God says, "Jesus Christ is the same yesterday and today and forever" (NIV). So I would choose to believe that His love for me and His life in me had not changed, but were still as warm and true and certain as before.

How I missed my sister! I remember going out under the sky at night to decisively tell the Lord (and myself), "I don't *have* to see Mary. You are enough." Again He would meet the longings of my heart, but it wasn't with the easy joy I'd so often known earlier.

I also experienced the reality that my husband couldn't meet all my needs. Dean loved me very much, but his love wasn't perfect. Sometimes he was occupied with his own needs. Sometimes he would be away for weeks at a time. Often the Spirit would bring to mind Psalm 73:25-26, reminding me again: "Only one Person is your best, your perfect life partner. Only One can be with you all the time and meet your deepest needs. You may love others as much as you can, as deeply as you will, but I must be your first love."

The truth of God's love and the solid footing of His Word kept me steady. I found that many truths I'd known in my head were becoming more deeply rooted in my life. The plowing time was of great value, and in the long run it made me love the Lord more.

But after about three years of plowing, God took me back to the second chapter of the Song of Solomon: "For lo, the winter is past, the rain is over and gone. The flowers appear on the earth; the time of singing has come, and the voice of the turtledove is heard in our land.... Rise up, my love, my fair one, and come away" (verses 12-13, NKJV). I felt God was telling me that the plowing time was over, the winter done with, and I now could look forward to a new fresh springtime of love with Him.

On the basis of Romans 15:32 ("That I may come unto you with joy by the will of God, and may with you be refreshed," KJV), I began to pray for increased refreshment in ministry. I trusted Him to fulfill in a new way John 7:38— that as His rivers of living water flowed through me in service to others, I, too, would experience more fully their life-giving freshness.

In His all-wise love, God still had more plowing times planned for me. Through each one He has strengthened my experience of His love. He has caused me to seek Him more desperately and know Him more deeply.

TRUEST GAIN

I've often appreciated the statement, "Each loss is truest gain if, day by day, He fills the place of all He takes away."

In our second missionary term we moved to Hong Kong, where Gene and Dean together directed the Navigator ministry. A year later, in 1959, we learned that Dean had cancer. He lived only nine more months.

It was a fast-growing form of cancer and quickly worsened, often causing him severe pain. We prayed, and others prayed. Twice, in direct answer to prayer, Dean experienced a dramatic turn for the better. But then God began to speak to our hearts, leading us no longer to claim healing and letting us know He wanted to take Dean home. He confirmed this by giving several men and women of God the same message. This affirmation helped us hold Dean in open hands and prepare our hearts for his homegoing.

Even in his suffering Dean would say, "Remember, Ruth, God has our best interests at heart." And God comforted both of us with a quotation someone sent us: "God is too wise to ever make a mistake and too loving to ever do anything unkind."

My friend Doug—the one who shared with me the sluggard verse from Proverbs—sent us Jeremiah 29:11. This time his choice of verses really appealed to me: "For I know the plans I have for you, says the LORD, plans for welfare and not for evil, to give you a future and a hope" (RSV). I had never focused on this verse before, but now I explored the full context while reading through the prophets. I discovered that history had proved this promise true for the people of God to whom it first was spoken. They suffered a great tragedy. Yet through it all, the Lord protected them and eventually restored their fortunes.

I went before God and said, "Lord, You say that You know the plans You have for us. I personally don't really know what You're doing. Dean is just starting his work in Asia. He has two young children. He has me. I don't understand what's happening or why You're allowing this. But You say Your plans are good, and You've never lied to me. So I choose to believe You." Again and again God used Jeremiah 29:11 to calm my heart and remove my fears.

More help came from Psalm 31:15, which says, "My times are in thy hand" (or as one version says, "My destiny is under Your control"). I realized that Dean's life was not in the hand of this dread disease. His life was not even in the hands of his doctor, a godly and skilled physician. Dean's life was in the hands of God. Our sovereign God was with us, and we could trust Him.

Gene and Mary took care of our children while I stayed

in the hospital room with Dean, sleeping in a smaller bed near his. Dean was growing weaker and was hardly able to speak. One morning as I woke up, he said to me in his slow speech, "You know, honey, I almost died last night."

"You did? No, I didn't know that."

His frail voice continued, "Oh, what a wonder it was!"

I tenderly urged him on. "Honey, what was a wonder?"

"Well…you just can't describe it."

"What was it you can't describe?"

Dean answered, "The wonder of being with the Lord." Then he began singing, and I joined him: "It will be worth it all when we see Jesus. Life's trials will seem so small when we see Christ. One look at His dear face, all sorrow will erase. So bravely run the race, till we see Christ."

Soon afterward, Dean's brave race was over and he went to be with the Lord. I had lost my best and primary human love. But I wasn't alone. I still had my first love; I still had my Source of deepest satisfaction. So the bottom did not fall out of my life.

I cried often. In my quiet times, no matter what I did, I would weep. I'd worship and cry. I'd pray and cry. I'd read the Bible and cry. But I also received rays of warmth from God, shafts of sunlight shining in through His Word, through other people, through other ways. For example, on the evening of the day Dean died, our daughter Doreen came rushing to me in the kitchen and said, "Just think, Mommy: My daddy can see the angels now!"

How grateful I was that God had taught me not to dare fixate on any other relationship, but to focus only on Him. Only His love was sure to be lifelong.

GOD SUPPLIES

Soon after Dean was promoted to glory I received a letter ending with these words: "May you find in the Lord Jesus Christ your Boaz." God was leading me to the book of Ruth as He had often done before. And what did Boaz do for Ruth? He satisfied her hunger and quenched her thirst; he provided her a home and supplied her needs; and he gave her a fruitful place in the harvest. I found the Lord doing these same things for me.

Six months after Dean's death, the children and I traveled back to the United States with Gene and Mary. After another six months we said good-bye to them as they returned to Asia. Then the three of us started a new chapter of our family life, settling in Colorado Springs. The children, especially Brian, struggled greatly, for they had lost not only their father but now also their extended family, including their Uncle Gene who was so much like their daddy. Despite their grief, Brian and Doreen adjusted quickly to their new surroundings, to school in America, and to life in general. How grateful I am for the many people who prayed for them back then and continued to do so throughout the years!

Besides providing prayer backers and friends, the Lord as my Boaz also supplied our needs for a home and clothing. And He gave me a part in His spiritual harvest at Glen Eyrie, headquarters of the Navigators. There I had abundant opportunities for ministry, including training other women to serve the Lord overseas. Besides counseling women and girls individually, I also spoke to women's groups and at conferences and retreats.

When we said good-bye to Gene and Mary, we hoped to join them later in Manila. But I had a deepening impression that the Philippines was not to be our field of service. I prayed about going back to Hong Kong, but again found no freedom of heart regarding this. Through counsel and prayer it seemed the Lord was telling me to stay at Glen Eyrie, helping train others who in turn would go into many places throughout the world.

But to think of perhaps never returning to Asia! Of perhaps never again ministering among the Chinese or Indians or Filipinos! Then I came across Deuteronomy 3:26-28.

God had told Moses he was not to enter the Promised Land. Moses pleaded with God to let him go. The Lord's reply was final: "Let it suffice you; speak no more to me of this matter.… But charge Joshua, and encourage and strengthen him: for he shall go" (RSV). Somehow this passage reaffirmed my conviction that, at least for the foreseeable future, we were to remain where we were. "You're not to go," I sensed the Lord saying, "and you're not to beg Me to let you go. Instead you're to charge others who will go and encourage and strengthen them." He graciously removed from my heart any restlessness about the matter.

HOLDING MY RIGHT HAND

I continued to be amazed at how God's love meets our needs when we let Him, satisfying our hearts and giving us contentment and joy. Soon after Dean's death my mother sent me a Scripture—Isaiah 41:13, which says, "For I, the LORD your God, will hold your right hand, saying to you, 'Fear not, I will help you' " (NKJV). *That's nice,* I had thought, especially in the version that says, "whispering to you, Fear not.…" Though the verse didn't touch my heart deeply at the time, I memorized it. Later I learned how much I needed it.

Brian and Doreen would often hold my hand, and that

meant a lot to me. I adored having them with me and enjoyed the sense this gave me of still being in a family. But I needed more than that. Especially in the second year after Dean passed away, the loneliness and longing for love often swept in upon me in a deeper way than before.

We were living in a lovely third-floor apartment in Glen Eyrie's huge old castle. How we reveled in the many opportunities for fun and rich fellowship with Navigator staff and trainees, especially at mealtimes. But overnight we would sometimes be the only people in the castle with its scores of rooms. I wasn't afraid of our being by ourselves. But at times in those still, silent hours after I tucked the kids into bed, and in my growing loneliness, a host of "what-if" fears about my life rose up. *What if God asks me to do this or that? What if such-and-such happens?* I'd even ask myself—while thinking about a man who was a good friend but whose wife I couldn't imagine being—*What if God asks me to marry him?*

So many different fears! "Lord," I would pray, "please say something to encourage me."

He would bring to me His promise in Isaiah 41:13, speaking it to my heart in the present tense: "I, the LORD your God, hold your right hand, whispering to you, 'Fear not, I will help you.' " As He spoke His Word to my heart,

I found it helpful not only to listen, but also to speak it back to Him in thankful prayer.

When the fears returned, I would say, "Tell me again."

I, the LORD your God, will hold your right hand....

"Lord," I responded, "I really need someone to hold my hand. And I have Someone: I have You! I've never had anyone better and I never will." Prayers like this kept me open to God and able to receive His love as He met my need.

I also discovered how much I wanted someone to tell me the words "I love you." Brian and Doreen said this often, but I longed for someone big to say it. The Lord often spoke of His love for me by reminding me of Isaiah 43:4—"You are precious in my eyes, and honored, and I love you" (RSV). I was to Him like a precious gem, which is loved not for its usefulness but for its great emotional value. I was honored in His eyes—amazing! And at any moment I could pause and let Him say, "I love you." I especially needed to pause like that in the summer.

Summer was the big conference season at Glen Eyrie, and there wasn't room for us in the castle. During those months each year we would rent a house in nearby Pleasant Valley, where my lonely times came more frequently.

Our neighbors one year included our Navigator friends Leroy and Virginia Eims. One beautiful summer evening I looked over, saw their home, and envisioned them inside happily together. "Virginia has Leroy," I began thinking, and I was tempted to complete the thought with "but I don't have anybody." However, I'd been warned that when I saw happy couples together I would be tempted with jealousy, so I had prayed about this and decided on a way to respond. I prayed, "Lord, give Leroy and Virginia a good evening. Bless them. Bless their relationship. And I thank You that I have You. Now tell me how You feel about me."

You are precious in My eyes, and honored, and I love you.

"Thank You, Lord, that I still have the best love I've ever had or ever will have."

These were the years when the red notebook you'll read about in Day 2 was filling up with God's personal words to me about Himself. I had started a new page with the heading "My _____," and had begun to fill the page with verses that actually used the word "my": my Rock, my Shepherd, my Champion, my Beloved, and so forth. I had settled on Psalm 16:5 in the Moffatt translation as my favorite verse for this page: "Thou art what I obtain from life, O thou Eternal, thou thyself art my share." My joy that God was "my Share in life" increased as I added Psalm 142:5, also from Moffatt: "I have thee as my very own, in the land of the living."

One summer I found myself focusing on God as my *Father.* I had a wonderful earthly father who loved me deeply, and I had always thought it was great to have God as my Father as well. But now, in this time of deeper loneliness, it meant so much more. I especially liked Romans 8:15 where J. B. Phillips, in place of "Abba, Father," says, "Father, my Father." I'd wake up in the morning thinking, "Father, my Father!" For the first time I was really taken with this thought. I imagined crawling onto His lap as a little girl and nestling in His arms as I spoke the words, "My Father!"

One morning, the day after we had moved from Glen Eyrie for the conference season, I woke up filled with low and lonely feelings. I started my quiet time, admitting to the Lord that I really didn't feel like having one. My Bible reading for that morning was Psalm 102. I came to these words: "I am like a pelican in the desert, like an owl moping in the ruins…like a lonely bird on the roof" (verses 6–7, Moffatt). Already I felt better—the psalmist had been even bluer than I was!

The passage goes on to say that God does not change. So I could say to Him, "Lord, You're the same as You were when I lived on the Glen. You're the same as You were when I lived with Dean. You are not the least bit different." I rejoiced as He comforted my heart with His unchanging love.

WHO NEEDS ME?

Four years after Dean died, we were surprised by the opportunity to finally return to Asia for the summer, including a month's stay with Gene and Mary in Manila. After the initial excitement, my heart was flooded with fears about going so far by ourselves and with anxiety about the many things that could happen to the children. I remembered all the sickness they had experienced there before. I also recognized that we would be in Satan's territory. Then Psalm 121:8 came forcibly to mind: "The LORD shall preserve your going out and your coming in from this time forth, and even forevermore" (NKJV).

Meanwhile, before we left Colorado Springs, several things happened that made me feel that no one there really needed me. Most of this was probably only in my imagination, though I think some of my impressions were accurate.

For Brian and Doreen, the month with their Uncle Gene and Aunt Mary in the Philippines was especially a delight. Since Gene was an identical twin to their father, being with him was almost like being with Daddy again. Gene did an incredible job of giving them a good time. And what a joy it was to have the whole clan together once more!

Later we stopped in Hong Kong, one of my favorite places. While there we visited a counselor, who was offering his services free of charge to missionaries (and I still quali-fied). After Dr. Rodd had talked with each of us, he told me Brian had some thoughts and feelings I might want to find out about.

As the children and I went out to dinner that night, Brian hesitantly mentioned that there was something he should probably let me know.

"What is it, Brian?"

"Well," he answered, "I don't think I should tell you. It might make it hard for you to be a good mother."

"Oh," I said, "honey, please tell me. Mommy will un-derstand."

Finally he came out with it: "You know…sometimes I wish you would die so I could go live with Uncle Gene."

I handled it without tears as long as I was with the chil-dren. "Honey," I told him, "I can understand that. He's a wonderful uncle. He's so much like your daddy. I under-stand why you feel that way."

But in bed that night I let myself have a long, hard cry: Even my kids didn't need me!

I knew this was a lie. Brian didn't mean he didn't need me. But that's the feeling I had.

The Lord lifted me from that experience to thrill me in a new way with what I mean to Him. I recognized the truth that if God were to take me home any moment, He would lovingly meet the needs of those around me in other ways. The fact is, most of us are probably needed here much less than we like to think. But for all of time and all eternity, there's an exciting sense in which God does "need" you and me. In one sense He has no needs. But in another sense He has love needs. He has longings. And we as His loved ones can fulfill His deep desire for intimacy with us through our love and worship, our fellowship, our obedience. This quotation captured that truth for me: "Every soul is a vast reservoir from which God can receive eternal pleasure." Each of us can bring Him joy in ways no one else can. And that will never change.

FROM IMPOSSIBLE TO WONDERFUL

Someone has said, "When God wants to do something wonderful, He begins with a difficulty. When He wants to do something very wonderful, He begins with an impossibility."

After another four years went by, the Lord led me to marry again. Warren Myers—who served in Asia during the same years Dean and I did—became my husband and the head of our family, warmly welcomed by our teenagers (though, of course, adjustments followed). That's the "very wonderful" part. The "impossibility" is how Warren and I were brought together. For years I had a profound respect for his walk with God, and I greatly valued his friendship. Yet when Warren told me he felt the Lord wanted us to begin a relationship, I thoroughly disagreed.

The years went by. I'm sure it took clever strategy on the Lord's part to keep Warren unmarried, especially with lovely, godly women available and despite unrelenting encouragement from friends to find a wife. I prayed that God would lead Warren to someone else. How grateful I am the Lord disregarded those prayers. As Hannah More, a British author and playwright in the early 1800s, wrote, "Did not God sometimes withhold in mercy what we ask, we would be ruined at our own request."

Warren had been twenty-three when he yielded his life to Christ as Lord. At that time God assured him that if he left marriage in His hands, He would not let him miss the right girl or marry the wrong one. Now, twenty-three years later, God answered by working in my heart in a thorough way. He gradually transformed my respect for Warren into love, eradicated my objections, and gave me a deep desire to become his wife.

Once again I knew I dared not hold this earthly love with a clenched hand. After all, Warren was God's man, not mine. So even before we finalized our engagement, I promised to give Warren back to the Lord all the days of his life. I included that promise in my wedding vows.

A year and a half after Warren and I were married, we returned to Asia, where we have lived and ministered for most of our married life. For three years we had Brian and Doreen with us in Singapore, for twenty-three years they were half a world away.

Then in 1995 Warren was diagnosed with cancer—fourth-stage lymphoma. In the months and years since we learned this, he has been prayed for by the elders of our church (James 5:14-16) and by many others around the world, and he has undergone careful and promising treatment. With confidence we ask for complete healing, believing this fits in with our much deeper desire and prayer, "Our Father who art in heaven, may Your name be honored, may Your kingdom come, may Your will be done." We have a quiet faith that the Lord is healing him. Yet we refuse to clench our fingers around physical healing, unwilling to let go.

I want Warren to be healed. I want him to live a long time, and I believe he will. But more than that I want God's will. He knows the good plans He has for us, plans for welfare and not for evil, to give us a future and a hope. I thank the Lord for this promise, and I believe it because He's never lied to me.

DEEP ROOTS IN THE SOIL OF HIS LOVE

In the decades of living I've outlined here, I've seen God beginning to answer for me Paul's beautiful prayer for believers in Ephesians 3:17-19 (expressed here in *The Living Bible*):

> *May your roots go down deep into the soil of God's marvelous love; and may you be able to feel and understand, as all God's children should, how long, how wide, how deep, and how high his love really is; and to experience this love for yourselves, though it is so great that you will never see the end of it or fully know or understand it. And so at last you will be filled up with God himself.*

This may sound like an impossibly high goal—to be "filled up with God Himself" and to fully experience a love that's so far beyond fully knowing. But it's not too hard for God. Immediately Paul goes on to say, "Now glory be to God, who by His mighty power at work within us is able to do far more than we would ever dare to ask or even dream of—infinitely beyond our highest prayers, desires, thoughts, or hopes." If we truly want to know His love more, we can use this prayer of Paul's to pour out our hearts to Him, and He will more than answer.

God offers us a perfect and permanent love, a love relationship that can meet our deepest needs at every point of life and forever. And He wants us to respond to His love. In His heart He is intensely involved with us.

I wonder, are we intensely involved with Him? Only as we daily renew our focus on Him as our first love, our best love, our perfect love, can we find the peace that comes with a satisfied heart.

I Must Have Love

Through the years, the Lord has been weaving into my life a richer awareness of how lavishly He loves me (and all of us) and how deeply He longs for each of us to experience His love. My heart has been opened again and again to delightful discoveries that have made me feel more satisfied and at rest in Him, more alive in His love, more liberated, more secure.

All of these rich discoveries are available to anyone who truly wants to know God better.

A. W. Tozer wrote of the knowledge of God stretching out before us like a vast ocean, with you and me like children playing along the beach (and, I like to add, perhaps dipping our toes into the water now and then). There's *so much more* to know and experience of this wonderful, loving God. We've only just begun.

Amy Carmichael, Irish missionary to India, deeply experienced the love of God. Yet in one of her poems she implored Him to reveal His love even more:

Love of my heart, my stream runs dry;
 O Fountain of the heavenly hills,
Love, blessed Love, to Thee I cry,
 Fill all my secret hidden rills.
Waters of Love, O pour through me;
 I must have Love; I must have Thee.

I'm trusting that you've begun to read this book because you have this same longing deep within, even as I do: We *must* have love. We must have *God's* love. We must have *God,* the only source of perfect, unfailing love, the only one who can fully satisfy our hearts. I believe God has sovereignly brought you and me together at this time and through these pages, and He wants to bless us in the adventure of letting Him respond to our heart cry.

The Lord deeply desires for us to know Him and experience His love. With boundless emotional longing, He wants us to know Him as He really is. He has already handed us an invitation to this in His Word, where we find the fullest portrait of Him, the most complete unveiling of His love, ready for us to contemplate and experience. From beginning to end, and in surprising and heartwarming ways, the Bible reveals a love that can flood our hearts with ever-increasing power through the Holy Spirit within us. God's love is a love that entirely satisfies, a love that brings true happiness and inner growth. It's a love that expands and corrects our thinking, changing us both inside and out.

Psalm 90 is a prayer of Moses as he led the people of Israel in the wilderness. They had known many sins, many failures. But Moses knew the Lord well, and in verse 14 he prays to Him, "Satisfy us in the morning with your steadfast love, so that we may rejoice and be glad all our days" (NRSV). The Moffatt translation reads, "Let thy love dawn on us undimmed." Moses knew the true source of all satisfaction: the Lord's steadfast love, dawning in our darkness. He knew this was the basis for joy even in the hard times. And he asked to experience it early.

I've found this Scripture a helpful one to pray. *Lord, do this for me: Satisfy me early, soon, this morning, with Your steadfast love, so I can rejoice and be glad all day long.* Then I pray the same thing for my husband and for us as a couple: *Satisfy us early with Your love.* And I gradually spread out from there, praying for others: *Satisfy them (or him or her) this morning with Your steadfast love. Let Your love dawn on them this morning, so that today they may rejoice in You.*

God has given us in His Word a beautiful picture of what His steadfast love is like. He wants to speak His love to our hearts, individually, tenderly. He wants you to take time to hear His words of love and to let them dawn on you undimmed, that you may very soon be satisfied…and be glad all your days.

Dear Lord, I thank You that I am Yours, that You know me through and through, and that it's no accident You've led me to this book.

Father, I've tasted Your love, and I long to experience more deeply how You really feel about me. I long to know in my daily life the intense reality and great wonder of Your boundless love, which You so freely bestow on those who seek You.

Help me turn away from my misconceptions of Your love and from being casual or indifferent toward You. Help me to turn from hectic, frantic activity that often makes even my time with You so hurried. I ask that through Your Word You will speak to me of Your perfect love in powerful, life-changing ways.

I pray in Jesus' name…

God's words of love for me today:
Psalms 86:15; 90:14; 100:5; 118:1; 1 John 4:16

In the space below, write out the verse or phrase from these passages that helps you most. You can follow this same encouraging step for all thirty-one days.

He Can More Than Satisfy Me

"This is real love," we read in 1 John 4:10. "It is not that we loved God, but that he loved us and sent his Son as a sacrifice to take away our sins" (NLT). This is real love. This is where we find the kind of love we most deeply need—not in human relationships, but in God. If we want real love, ideal love, perfect love, God's heart is where to find it. It's the only love big enough to meet the deep needs in your life and mine.

Indeed God can and will go *beyond* merely meeting those needs. "God is so vastly wonderful," wrote A. W. Tozer in *The Pursuit of God,* "so utterly and completely delightful, that He can without anything other than Himself meet and overflow the deepest demands of our total nature, mysterious and deep as that nature is." These are words I return to again and again, for I've found them true. Down through the years, in a countless variety of circumstances in every season of life, God has proven to me that He can more than satisfy my heart—*as I let Him.*

The Lord can meet our every need because He is a God of perfect, overflowing love that has no limits. It's hard to know where to start in describing God's love. From beginning to end the Bible tells us how He feels about us. Many verses state specifically what His love is like. Also, in passage after passage we can discern this love through His actions or words, as we learn to look for clues—just as we do on the human level when we like someone and try to find out whether he or she likes us. In the Bible those clues are everywhere.

As a widow with two young children during the months and years that followed my first husband's death from cancer at age thirty-two, I became more diligent than ever in seeking to know God and experience His love in new ways. (Trials have a way of driving us onward like that, don't they?) I bought a red notebook that I used only for recording truths about God. In the top corner on the front side of each sheet I wrote down some word or fact about God, something He would impress upon me through my times with Him: Refuge, Hiding Place, Power, Love, Strength, Bridegroom, Bread of Life, and so forth. On the front page for each topic I wrote out verses the Holy Spirit had used to grip my heart. Then I could go back to them again and again for refreshment and praise and thanksgiving.

Some of the entries were a full verse, others just a phrase. I wrote each one in whatever Bible version I liked best for that particular passage and sometimes partly in one version, partly in another. I also memorized many of these rich verses.

Often a verse would impress me mentally but I wouldn't yet feel it was truly mine. It had not yet deeply touched my heart. So I would record the reference on the back of the page. Then later I could dig deeper into it, letting the Spirit make it real to my heart. Also on the back of the page I added poems or quotes or devotional thoughts relating to the topic.

The notebook grew to be quite thick. In times when I really needed a dose of God's love (or His peace or strength or whatever), I could open those pages and run back to Scriptures already full of meaning, truths He had spoken personally to me. And in those times of need they became lifesavers.

It helped so much to seek God diligently like this. I wish I could say that I've sought Him just as diligently every day and in every quiet time. I've gone through many times of dissatisfaction and unmet longings because I wasn't letting Him satisfy me. Still He has been faithful to answer prayer, bringing me back to His personal love again and again and keeping it a major theme in my life. (You'll find a fuller account of this in the section "My Story: First Love" earlier in this book.)

One of the most helpful quotes I came across during those years as a widow was something written by Hudson Taylor, pioneer missionary in China. He was facing the death of his dearly loved wife, Maria, and his children were all in school in faraway England. In this lonely time he found great refreshment through John 7:37, where Jesus invites anyone who is thirsty to come to Him and drink. "Who does not thirst?" Taylor wrote. "Who has not mind-thirsts or heart-thirsts, soul-thirsts or body-thirsts? Well, no matter which, or whether I have them all, *Come unto Me and...*remain thirsty? Ah no! *Come unto Me and drink!*

"What?" Taylor continued. "Can Jesus meet my need? Yes, and more than meet it. No matter how intricate my path, how difficult my service; no matter how sad my bereavement, how far away my loved ones; no matter how helpless I am, how deep are my soul yearnings; Jesus can meet all—all, and more than meet."

Father, thank You for the lasting intensity of Your overflowing, never-ending love. Thank You that Your love is utterly reliable and delightful, that it is so much better than anything I could imagine or hope for in life.

I praise You, Lord, that You are so vastly wonderful, so utterly and completely delightful, that You can meet and overflow the deepest needs of my total nature, mysterious and deep as that nature is.

Show me clearly and continually how to respond to You. Today, and every day, enable me to direct my yearnings toward You, to come to You with my inner thirsts—and drink.

In Jesus' name…

God's words of love for me today:
John 7:37; Psalms 37:3-8; 52:8; 89:14-16;
103:1-5; 1 John 4:9-10

The Lord Is All I Need

One of my favorite psalms for starting my quiet time in a fresh way has long been Psalm 63. David wrote this psalm when he was in the desert of Judah. There in the wilderness he prayed, "O God, you are my God, earnestly I seek you; my soul thirsts for you, my body longs for you, in a dry and weary land where there is no water" (NIV).

Yet only a few lines later David wrote, "My soul is satisfied" (NASB). He was satisfied not because he had escaped from the desert, but because of God's love and presence: "Your lovingkindness is better than life" (verse 3). He knew that nothing in his physical situation could meet his deep needs—his "heart-thirsts" and "soul-thirsts," as Hudson Taylor described them.

Over time, we go to God with such an assortment of needs and inadequacies and emergencies: time and work pressures, marriage difficulties, rebellious or straying children, bereavement, financial problems, emotional problems, problems with other people, lost jobs, lost friends, lost happiness. We're in a dry and weary land, and we're thirsty. Even in our best times you and I have vast inner needs—the deep demands of our mysterious and deep nature, as A. W. Tozer put it. But God knows all those mysteries within us and all their depths, and He meets each one with a love that is great beyond measure.

After all, *He* designed you and me, mysterious inner needs and all. His masterly design includes having our deepest needs met only by Him. Only He can fill the God-shaped vacuum within us, as the great scientist and philosopher Blaise Pascal described it. That vacuum includes, for example, a deep inner need to *adore:* to love and be devoted to someone we can admire totally, always and forever, without the slightest reservation—someone who will never change, who will never disappoint us or fail us.

We often try to fill this vacuum with our spouse, our children, our friends, or other people who mean so much to us. But sooner or later they all let us down in one way or another. After all, they're imperfect and limited just as we are, and they have their own human needs to attend to. We end up disillusioned. But is it fair to expect anyone or anything else to give us what only our perfect, all-sufficient God is able to give?

I'm not discrediting human love. Earthly relationships can be beautiful, and God has used them continually in my life as an expression of His love for me. But as one Christian counselor said, when two people try to find ideal and perfect love from each other, it's like two paupers trying to borrow from one another. Neither has much to give; both remain unsatisfied.

I like Psalm 16:2,5 in the *New Century Version*: "Every good thing I have comes *from you*.... The LORD is all I need." The more we let God be God in our lives, the more we find that He is the answer to what we're lacking, the answer to what we're longing for. Our needs and our trials give Him a chance to reveal Himself in new ways. For every need in our emotional or mental or spiritual life, for every problem in our relationships, for every trial we go through, God offers something (such as His love, His power, His provision) that can bring us through triumphantly—if we know and believe and count on Him in the hour of need. God is our first Source, and ultimately the only Source, of all we need for a full and satisfied life.

And we have such a great advantage in this relationship

with God because it's *internal.* Every other love is limited by some degree of distance and by the barriers imposed by our physical bodies. But God dwells within us, so that our relationship with Him has unlimited potential for constant closeness and joy and fulfillment.

Here indeed is love.

Father, I worship You because of who You are—a God who understands me and faithfully takes care of me, a God of intense and ardent affection for me that will last for all time and eternity.

I praise You that for every need of my heart and every situation in my life there is something in You that can meet my deepest need, and that You are here within me to do so.

I pray that Your love will dawn on me undimmed, so that I may rejoice and be glad in You. And may my roots go deeper and deeper into the soil of Your marvelous love. Day by day, hour by hour, fill me with Yourself.

God's words of love for me today:
1 Chronicles 29:10-13; Psalms 13:5-6; 16:2,5,11; 63:1-3;
Isaiah 41:10; Ephesians 3:16-20

I Am God's Eternal Longings Coming True

There was a time when I was troubled by the command that Jesus says is first and greatest—that we should love the Lord our God with all our heart and soul and mind and strength. It made me feel uncomfortable and guilty. I wanted to love God this much, and I liked to think I sometimes did. Yet I knew I didn't love Him that way all the time, and perhaps I never really offered Him such love at all. Oh, I loved Him more than I loved anyone else, but love Him with *all* my heart and soul and mind and strength? No, I was so often distracted or distrustful or drifting.

Then I began to realize that this is the most flattering

and complimentary verse in the Bible. I am so important to God that He wants *me* to love Him totally. We don't approach strangers on the street and say, "Please love me with all your heart!" They would think we were crazy, and they'd probably be right. Only if someone means a great deal to us, only if we really love that person, do we ask that. And it's what God has asked from us. This wonderful Person—the supreme Ruler of the universe, Creator of all things, the One possessing all power and exalted far above all, the most desirable of all persons—*He* asks me to love Him with all my heart. He tells you and me, "This is what I want from you first of all, more than anything else."

Why is our love so important to God? Why does He care so much whether or not we love Him? I think it's because He has always been a relational God. He was never a lonely, solitary figure somewhere out in eternity, all alone in the empty reaches of space. He has always been a triune God in intimate relationship—the Father, Son, and Holy Spirit in loving communion. And before time began God decided He wanted to include many others in that circle of love.

God is always yearning for us and always has been. We read in Ephesians 1:4 that before the foundation of the world He chose us in Christ. Throughout Ephesians we find a heartwarming picture of His eternal longing, His Father's heart for us, tender and loving and full of gracious intentions. He longed for children, for a family of His own. He longed to have a bride for His Son, a bride on whom He could lavish His love. He longed for a temple in which His Holy Spirit could dwell, for people on earth who could share with Him an intimacy far surpassing any human relationship. He longed for a people to be His very own.

Looking ahead from eternity past He envisioned a relationship with us that would embody the many-faceted delights He would later build into human relationships— the tenderness of a father with his child, the comfort and stimulation of friendship, the supreme joys of bride and bridegroom. And as He planned His own family, God chose you and me to belong to Him. We are God's eternal longings coming true.

God is wrapped up in mankind. He has been reaching out for personal involvement with people from the beginning of Genesis, and He continues to reach out. Through the centuries He has found delight in all those who would, by faith, turn to Him. He referred to Abraham as His friend. He called David a man after His own heart. His eyes search the whole earth, looking for people who will let Him demonstrate His love to them. He is eager to show it in special ways to anyone who will be wholly His, to anyone who will *respond.*

Dear Lord, thank You that I'm so important to You, so valuable, that You ask me to love You with all my heart and soul and mind and strength. I praise You that You always have been and always will be intimately relational. I thank You for the honoring truth that I am Your eternal longing coming true. How amazing that, as a father with his child and as a bridegroom with his bride, You exult over me with joy, taking great delight in me!

May Your Spirit flood my heart with how You feel about me and how deeply You are committed to me. In fresh, new ways assure me that Your love for me is intensely personal, overflowing, and never-ending—the one and only perfect love.

I pray in Jesus' name...

God's words of love for me today:
Matthew 25:34; Mark 12:28-31;
Ephesians 1:3-6; Zephaniah 3:17; Revelation 21:1-4

His Love for Me Is Intensely Personal

God's love is not simply for mankind as a mass. It's not some sentimental, vague, diffused feeling, as the comic strip character Charlie Brown expressed: "I love mankind. It's people I can't stand." No, God really likes individual people. His love is intensely personal.

Jesus showed this on earth as He concentrated on individuals. He showed no partiality, no tinge of preference for any particular size or color or talent or educational level or social status. He loved individuals impartially, yet intensely, showing us what God is like.

The Cross gives us the greatest unveiling of God's personal love. After all, He did not send His Son to die just for mankind as a mass. In Galatians 2:20 Paul speaks of how

Christ the Son of God "loved *me* and gave himself for *me*" (NIV). Out of His infinite capacity to focus on each individual person, God died for *me* personally and for *you* personally. His love is not just for the sum of humanity or even just for the church as a whole. Toward each of us it's a personal love for His precious child.

You and I have only a limited number of people we can know, much less devote time to and love in an intensely personal way. God has no such limit on His ability to love or His availability. With infinite capacity He can and does love you as though you were the only person who ever lived on this earth. This is what first won me to Him as a child, on the night my mother turned my attention to John 3:16 after sensing my troubled spirit. As Paul wrote in Galatians 2:20, the Son of God loved *me* and gave Himself for *me.* God's love and His gift are personal.

God's relationship with us is already something He cherishes, and it will reach perfection in the eternal future. It will be an everlasting revel of delight for both Him and us. As I've imagined being before His throne with those vast millions of believers, I've sometimes had a wistful feeling that I'll just be part of a crowd. Then I remember that even now He can zero in on me and give me intimate, delightful, personal fellowship with Himself. How much more true will this be when I'm fully in His presence with all His loved ones? We won't be disappointed. As C. S. Lewis wrote, "The happiness God has designed for His higher creatures is an ecstasy of love and delight with Himself and one another, compared with which the most rapturous love between a man and a woman on this earth is mere milk and water."

By choosing to love us in this intense and personal way, God has made Himself vulnerable. "God has bound up His happiness with ours," Tozer wrote, "and He'll never know unmixed happiness again until His work in us is finished and we're all gathered home." His pleasure is linked with ours: We can grieve Him (hurting ourselves in the process), or we can bring Him delight as we enjoy satisfying His longings for our love.

Wonderful God, how amazing it is that Your love for me is so intensely personal!

I thank You especially for all that Your love for me has cost You—for the agony You felt as You watched Your Son suffer and die for me when I was a stranger to You, and an enemy.

To think that Your Son *loved me* and *gave Himself* for *me*—what a costly and convincing way to show how intense and personal Your love is. How I praise and thank You, Lord, that the key to living close to You is not how much I love you, for my love is but a shallow stream compared to Your love for me. How I rejoice that I can live close to You because Your love for me is a shoreless, bottomless sea!

Lead me, loving Lord, to passages in Your Word that will fill me with a deeper love for You. Then may they become beautifully polished jewels as I meditate on them and let Your Holy Spirit reveal their truth more clearly and more deeply.

God's words of love for me today:

Psalm 17:6-7; Isaiah 57:15; Lamentations 3:22-23;

John 3:16; Galatians 2:20

Remember to record your answer to this question:

"What verse or phrase from these passages helps me most?"

How I Give God Pleasure

Perhaps you easily remember that God has compassion for you and is willing to help you. Or you may think of God as taking care of your needs in a somewhat condescending way—after all, we're His creatures, so He does His duty toward us. But maybe you've overlooked how intense His feelings really are—how He *desires* you, how much He finds delight whenever you cultivate your love relationship with Him.

When we overlook this truth, we rob God's love of the emotional content that the Scriptures portray. "For the LORD delights in you," God tells His people in Isaiah 62:4 (NASB). He loves us so much He will even serenade us: "He will take great delight in you; he will quiet you with his love, he will rejoice over you with singing," we read of Him in Zephaniah 3:17 (NIV). And Psalm 149:4 says, "The LORD takes pleasure in His people" (NASB).

I'm sure you're as astonished as I am that God can find such enjoyment from intimacy with us. An InterVarsity Press booklet, *The Quiet Time,* puts it this way:

> *That God desires our fellowship is one of the most amazing facts revealed in Scripture. The fact is so staggering that it's extremely difficult for us to grasp its meaning for us. That God should allow His creatures to have fellowship with Himself is wonderful enough. But that He can desire it, that it gives Him satisfaction and joy and pleasure, is almost too much for our understanding.*

This amazing love, so undeserved, is indeed difficult to grasp with our minds alone: God cares so intimately and personally about me that He longs for my fellowship. But as one poet has said, this truth of God's immeasurable love is "darkness to my intellect but sunshine to my heart."

You and I can actually bring God pleasure! As C. S. Lewis wrote, we can be "a real ingredient in the divine happiness…delighted in as an artist delights in his work or a father in a son." What better motivation can there be for spending time with Him day by day? When I get lukewarm or sidetracked by lesser pursuits (even in my quiet time), nothing does more to rekindle my heart than remembering how much the Lord desires fellowship with me.

At times we may have to honestly confess, "Lord, I don't feel like having my quiet time this morning, but my purpose is still the same: I want to know You and bring You pleasure." Amy Carmichael prayed, "O Lord Jesus, my Beloved, may I be a joy to You." This is a prayer God continually answers, as much as we allow Him to.

So we can let the words from Song of Solomon 2:13-14 draw us to Him. In *The Berkeley Version* they read, "Arise, my love, my beauty, and come along with me…. Let me hear your voice, let me see your face; for your voice is sweet, and your face is lovely."

What? Me, Lord? Are You sure You have the right number? I mean, I remember what an awful attitude I had just last night. I can name a long list of things about me that I know are far from attractive. But You say my voice is sweet to Your ears? And my face is beautiful?

"Yes," He says, "for I've made you a new person in

Christ. Deep in the inner core of your being you're a brand-new person, and you're beautiful to me, and I love to hear your voice."

Lord, I don't understand how this could be—but it feels good! It warms my heart. Say it again, I want to hear more....

"Rise up, my *love,* my *fair one,* and come away...."

We bring God joy simply by responding to Him, by taking time with Him as His loved one, His fair one, to sit at His feet and let Him speak to us His words of love.

How easily we forget what an honored privilege it is to offer our personal worship to God. When you go before Him and worship Him, you give Him what no one else in the universe can give: your own personal love, your own personal adoration, your own personal response to Him. Joy comes when you respond to your heavenly Father with your unique personality, which He created—when you take to heart His Word and tell Him your feelings and your love. And He is grieved when you don't respond.

God uniquely fashioned each one of us for Himself. He didn't follow some pattern or mass-production mold. No, He wanted a variety of people because the love coming from each of us satisfies Him in a different way, helping to complete His joy in being our Father, our Beloved, our Friend.

Each of us is individually precious to Him and will be for all eternity. Each of us can give Him the intimacy He longs for, the intense pleasure and satisfaction of our unique ways of relating to Him.

The following quotation captures that truth for me: "Every soul is a vast reservoir from which God can receive eternal pleasure." You are that, and I am that. As we love God and relate to Him, He drinks with pleasure from the waters of our love.

Dear Father, I'm so glad that You like me as well as love me and that You desire me and delight in me.

Thank You for the amazing truth that my soul is a vast reservoir from which You can receive eternal pleasure.

Because You find pleasure in me, I ask You to help me please You more fully and not grieve You. Enable me to bring You joy day by day as I relate to You with a responsive heart and let Your love satisfy me.

God's words of love for me today:
Psalms 147:10-11; 149:4-5; Song of Songs 2:10,14;
Romans 12:1-2; Hebrews 13:20-21

I Am His Treasure

We are God's treasure! This is one of the most exciting truths in the Bible, and it came alive for me one July in the cool, beautiful mountains of Malaysia.

My husband and I had traveled there from our home in Singapore to enjoy a vacation and do some writing. Again and again in my quiet time I found myself distracted with thoughts about a book we were writing. The creative juices (whatever they are) would flow, and new ideas or fresh ways of saying old ones would keep coming. How could I help but write them down? After all, each one seemed like a special treasure that could so easily be lost. Often the inspirations were thoughts about the Lord—but if I wrote too much, might those ideas not actually end up being a rival to Him? Or even worse, an idol! It seemed so.

So I prayed, "Lord, more and more may I be taken up

with You as my treasure. And may I see more clearly that I'm a treasure to You, created to bring You joy." I asked that He would be central in my time with Him in a special way, that He would rein my thoughts in, and that I would write just enough to aid my praise for Him, my communion with Him, and my prayers for others.

On those days my meditations focused on the amazing fact that God takes special delight in each of us as His own priceless possession, cherishing us and guarding us and looking out for our best interests.

The Bible also tells us that God is *our* treasure, *our* inheritance—our portion, the best life can offer us now and forever (Psalm 73:25-26). As A. W. Tozer wrote, "The man who has God as his treasure has all things in one, and he has it purely, legitimately, and forever." In view of God's power and majesty and tender love, this statement is easy to understand.

But that *we* are *His* inheritance, *His* treasure—isn't this incredible?

The Living Bible puts it this way: "Because of what Christ has done, we have become gifts to God that he delights in.... God has been made rich because we who are Christ's have been given to him!" (Ephesians 1:11,18). Other Scriptures confirm the truth that we are God's special treasure, a source of delight to Him. God looks at us and thinks, *"He* belongs to Me…*she* belongs to Me. I am so rich!" We are gifts that Jesus has given Him—and very special gifts too. We're just what He always wanted! As Tozer said, we are more valuable to Him than galaxies of newly created worlds.

"You are precious in my eyes," God says to His people in Isaiah 43:4 (RSV), "and honored, and I love you."

Me? Precious and honored in God's eyes? He's the Most High God, exalted above all; *He* is honored, and we stand in awe of Him. So how can He say that I am honored?

In the Moffatt translation, Isaiah 43:4 reads, "So precious are you to me, so honoured, so beloved." *So* honored? That's what I am to Him? It doesn't make sense, but it's true. You and I have been brought to the place of highest privilege. God Himself honors and favors us.

When we realize we're that important to God, it does something to how we think about ourselves. Not that it makes us proud. Pride means we take credit for who we are. But God wants to see us hold our heads high in thankfulness because we know He loves us and has made us members of His royal family and heirs of all things with Christ. He gets all the credit. It is He who made us; it is He who brought us to Christ and purified us; it is He who has given us new life in His presence, now and forever.

Throughout all eternity we'll bring Him joy. We'll be His jewels, His "prized possession," His "special possession" (Malachi 3:17, Moffatt and RSV). We'll be "a crown of beauty…and a royal diadem" in the hand of our God (Isaiah 62:3, NASB)—a treasure He will hold close to His heart, a crown He'll lift high to show His magnificent handiwork. For eternity we'll be a glory to our Designer and Maker.

Father, I worship before You as my Treasure, my Inheritance, the best that life can offer me both now and forever. And I come to You deeply thankful— and amazed—that I belong to You as Your special treasure and prized possession—that I am a unique and valued gift that Jesus has given to You.

My heart is overwhelmed with gratefulness and delight that You bestow honor on me, honor that is eternal and unchanging. How grateful I am that earthly honor fades into insignificance in the light of the honor that comes from You—that I no longer need to seek honor from people because I already have the greatest of all honors. I'm so glad I can trust You to take care of the favor-and-honor department of my earthly life, with perfect love and wisdom.

Work in me today by Your mighty power and love, enabling me to offer You a foretaste of the joy that I will bring You throughout all eternity.

In Jesus' name…

God's words of love for me today:

Malachi 3:16-17; John 3:16-17; Ephesians 1:11-13,18; 2:4-7; 1 Peter 2:9-10; Colossians 1:12; 3:12

Even Now, He
Treasures Me

God doesn't wait until eternity to treasure us. He treasures us now in spite of our warts and wrinkles and blemishes. We're chosen ones, holy and beloved, honored in His eyes today, and bringing Him joy as we worship Him and walk with Him and talk of Him to each other.

Even now we're just as near to God and dear to God as Jesus is! In the first chapter of Ephesians we read that He has made us welcome into the same everlasting love He bears toward His Beloved Son. And Jesus, in His high priestly prayer in John 17, said that the Father loves us in the same way He loves His Son. A wonderful old hymn sets forth these truths:

So near, so very near to God,
Nearer I could not be,
For in the person of His Son
I'm just as near as He.

So dear, so very dear to God,
I could not dearer be;
The love wherewith He loves the Son,
Such is His love to me.

God gives many illustrations to show how precious we are to Him. As He delighted to be among His people of old, dwelling in the temple at Jerusalem, so now He delights in us who are His temple, His dwelling place (Ephesians 2:21-22).

Think of how parents treasure each newborn child, marveling at the handiwork of God, at the tiny, perfect toes and fingers; how they envision the inner person ready to unfold; and later how they rejoice at each stage of growth. So our heavenly Father treasures us. We have been born into His family; we are really and truly His children, loved with a deep, unchanging love (1 John 3:1-2).

As an artist treasures each masterpiece he produces

(imagine how Michelangelo must have treasured his statues of Moses and David, and how Monet must have treasured his cathedral paintings, each with different lighting, a different impression, and each so beautiful)—so God treasures each of us as His work of art, one of His masterpieces, both naturally and spiritually (Psalm 139:13-15; Ephesians 2:10).

And the illustration I like best is the bridegroom and bride. "As a bridegroom rejoices over his bride, so will your God rejoice over you" (Isaiah 62:5, NIV). In the Song of Solomon it's the bridegroom we hear calling, "Rise up, my love, my fair one, and come away." As a couple in love treasures each other—as a groom delights in his bride—so the Lord, as our inner and eternal Life Partner, treasures us.

The Lord takes special pleasure in us as we respond to Him with love, worship, faith, and obedience. As we let Him be our chief treasure, we bring Him unique joys that no one else can bring. And we bring Him unique griefs when we ignore Him and speed through our days, giving Him little thought. Day by day, moment by moment, you and I determine whether He loves us with a glad love or a grieved love.

Why does God so long to be our treasure and our first love? Because we are *His* treasure, His eternal longings coming true, and therefore He wants only the best for us. He created us so that our lives operate best when (and only when) we let Him be our treasure.

Heavenly Father, I thank You that at this very moment You treasure me and that You love me now in the same everlasting way that You love Your Beloved Son Jesus.

You are worthy—infinitely worthy—of my love, my worship, my faith, and my obedience. How I long to constantly claim You as my chief treasure. May my love for You grow so that day by day, moment by moment, You may love me with a glad love rather than a grieved love.

God's words of love for me today:

Psalm 139:13-16; John 17:23,26; Ephesians 2:10; 2:19-22;

Colossians 1:13; 1 John 3:1-2

He Draws Me Near

Because you are a special treasure to God, He is working to draw you into a deeper love for Him—away from any idols in your life, away from rival interests, away from giving first place to His good gifts instead of to Him.

In Jeremiah 31:3 the Lord tells His people, "I have loved you with an everlasting love; therefore with lovingkindness I have drawn you" (NKJV). Every hour since you first met Him, He has been pursuing you, seeking to draw you closer as a mother draws her child, as a bridegroom his bride. He wants you *near.*

I've found through the years that He draws us in many ways. He wants us to understand the ways He does this, so that we can be responsive to them and enjoy a closer, richer relationship with Him. In the portrait of the Lord and His beloved in Song of Songs 1:4, the bride entreats Him, "Draw me after you, and let us run together" (NASB). Isn't this a tender, meaningful prayer? *Draw me after You and let us run together—today! All day long! And every day.*

And how does He draw us?

I believe He grants all of us certain love-gifts that help us move closer to Him and know Him better. Five of these stand out to me as foundational to our love relationship with Him.

The first love-gift is His Word, where we find our most beautiful and comprehensive portrait of Him. As we take time to read and listen, He keeps telling us there—from cover to cover and in a multitude of ways—not only that He loves us, but also how and why and how much. Often He does this by plainly declaring His love and by plainly telling what He is like. But beyond this, everything in Scripture helps us know Him better if that's truly what we seek and if we let His love-truths soak in. The narrative stories, for example, reveal so much about God as they record His dealings with people (both individually and in groups). Just as we get to know a fellow human being better by observing how he or she interacts with people, we learn about God through His involvement with people. The laws and commands in the Bible also reveal who the Lord is. They let us know what He stands for, the principles He delights in. They show His desire to lead us in paths that keep us from harm and assure our well-being as well as that of others, especially our children and spouses.

Another of God's love-gifts—His basic provisions to help us know Him better—is His indwelling presence through the Holy Spirit. As we feed on God's Word, the Spirit empowers us to see and understand the Lord and His love. He takes the truths about Jesus and makes them real to us in the core of our being, in the holy sanctuary deep within us. As a result, our knowledge of the Lord is more intimate than our knowledge of anyone else. He guides us into truth not just intellectually but by experience, by how He leads us to think and feel and choose. The Spirit Himself fills our hearts with God's love (Romans 5:5) so that it satisfies us and flows out to others.

The third love-gift that helps us know God and His love better is the body of Christ—other believers He places in our lives. In such special ways He reveals Himself to us through fellow Christ-followers—through pastors and teachers, counselors and mentors, as well as through those with less-obvious gifts. Whatever their spiritual gifts, we are enriched through them. And beyond this, we profit greatly from the way their lives reveal Christ. We see their faults; no one is a perfect channel of God's love. But we can also see the Lord in one another *if we want to*. We can choose to concentrate on Christ in them, making their strengths our major focus, rather than their flaws and failures. As we behold Christ in one another, He draws us closer to Himself.

The fourth basic provision, or love-gift, is simply the circumstances of daily life. God wants to enrich us through knowing Him better and becoming more like Him. To this end He arranges our days with the proper mixture of joys and trials, gains and losses, pleasure and pain. He holds our lives in the hollow of His hand, and into that place of security He brings the blessings and troubles we need: "I'll let this trial through," He says, "because it will strengthen her. No, not that one; it's more than she could bear right now." And, "I'll bestow that joy because it will help heal him, but not this one. Although he really wants this, it would hinder his spiritual growth."

These love gifts—God's Word, His Spirit, other believers, and the circumstances He allows or sends—draw us closer to Him. They help us stay on the path of obedience, which I think of as the fifth love-gift that helps us know God better. We can run through life with the Lord only when we choose His paths—the paths where He manifests His presence. He won't run with us on paths of disobedience. It's not that He'll forsake us, even as the sun does not forsake the earth when night falls or when thick clouds roll in. But if we aren't walking in His ways, God's presence won't be real to us. We won't enjoy the privilege of prayer (yet another love-gift) the way He desires; we won't know His warm, glad companionship.

So draw me after You, Lord, and let us run together. The image recalls the song, "My God and I go in the fields together; we walk and talk as good friends should and do. We clasp our hands, our voices ring with laughter. My God and I walk through the meadow's hue." Running with Him means pleasure and carefree enjoyment.

Running with God also includes running with perseverance the course marked out for us (Hebrews 12:1). We're running with One whose earthly race ended in a cross, and our own path includes the fellowship of His sufferings. This includes doing the difficult tasks He sends our way. I may fantasize that just around the corner life will become easy— just as soon as this or that particular commitment is over, this deadline met, this job done, and on and on. But according to Luke 9:23, will the day come when I won't have to deny myself to follow Him?

Do I even want such a day to come? My heart has been stirred by Phillips Brooks's poem:

Be strong.
We are not here to play, to dream, to drift.
We have hard work to do, and loads to lift.
Shun not the struggle; face it. 'Tis God's gift.

Draw me after You, dear Lord, and let us run together....

How I praise You, Lord, that You long for a closer relationship with me. How much I appreciate Your deep love for me and each love-gift You have bestowed on me so that I run close to You throughout my life. Enable me to say yes to running with You in carefree delight—and to running with perseverance, guided by Your Word and Your Spirit. Strengthen me as I run. Give me grace to trust You and say yes to paths of struggle and pain and disappointment whenever that's what You plan for me.

And give me grace, Lord, day by day, to seek You first and foremost—to faithfully set apart time to be alone with You. Enable me to say no (or not now) to secondary things that so easily crowd out time with You, and instead to choose Your special love-gifts first of all.

God's words of love for me today:

Psalm 119:64; Hosea 11:4; John 14:21,23;

Romans 8:28-29; Hebrews 4:15-16; 10:19-22

In All My Joys
and Trials

How glad I am that life is more than trials. Our God blesses each of His children lavishly. Isn't it true that when the Lord brings a super-special gift or event into our lives, it's not one lone mountaintop upon a bleak plain? Rather it's a high summit among a range of other majestic peaks. It's a refreshing oasis in a land of oases, not (at least spiritually) in an otherwise barren desert. How often, in His gracious will, He lets us live in a well-watered land filled with opportunities, special surprises, and rich relationships.

We're to receive these countless joys as special gifts of love: "Lord, this shows what Your heart for me is like—You love to do things that delight me! Thank You!" The gifts, all of them, should draw us nearer to the Giver. We're to freely enjoy them, but not clutch them.

Our son, Brian, helped us appreciate these lines by William Blake:

He who binds to himself a joy
Does the winged life destroy;
He who kisses the joy as it flies
Lives in eternity's sunrise.

We're meant to kiss our joys rather than clench them tightly and destroy them.

Kiss the joys gratefully and press on—onward to more joys but also to promised trials, all these together disclosing more of the Lord's loving design. As the hymn says,

Every joy or trial falleth from above,
Traced upon our dial by the Sun of love.

God is love, and all He says and does affirms this. How we rejoice when, in love, He shields us from obviously harmful things or brings unmistakably good things our way. Yet whatever He allows to touch our lives, seemingly good or bad, is an expression of His love and His desire for us.

Whatever He permits or sends is an invitation to draw closer to Him.

For years I've enjoyed Florence White Willett's poem that begins,

> *I thank God for the bitter things;*
> *They've been a friend to grace.*
> *They've driven me from the paths of ease*
> *To storm the secret place.*

The experience of trials—the taste, or more, of bitterness—often spurs us to let God love us. It makes us more aware of our needs, and it urges us to go to Him with them, seeking His presence and help.

In Hosea 2:14 the Lord says figuratively of His people, "I will allure her, and bring her into the wilderness, and speak tenderly to her" (RSV). Sometimes God must place us in the wilderness, setting us apart in a dry and thirsty land. He does this to draw us, allure us, and speak gently, kindly to our hearts.

Without trials, how would we really know how loving God is? What if we never faced loneliness or heartbreak, praying with empty hearts, "Lord, I need Your love"? Would we ever truly hear His reassurance that we're precious in His eyes, honored and deeply loved?

Without the assault of trials, how often would we run to hide in the shadow of His wings? David's prayer in Psalm 36 shows that this shelter is not like a cramped, dark, damp, meagerly stocked air-raid shelter. The Lord's refuge offers protection, but it offers so much more. It lets us feast on the abundance of His house, drink from His "river of delights," and enjoy the light of His presence.

Without trials as God's platform for revealing Himself, might we fail to experience the incredible greatness of His power in our personal lives? Just by reading about it in the Bible? That is essential. It gets the concept into our mind. But when we're caught in an impossible circumstance and cry out to Him and He answers with deliverance, then we know on a deeper level: Our God truly is powerful!

Apart from difficult circumstances, how earnestly would we seek Him? How deeply would we know Him? I'm sorry to say this, but isn't it true that you and I would soon be distracted and often forget Him if everything always went smoothly?

Dear Lord, thank You that You have permitted every trial in my life as a steppingstone to knowing Your love more intimately.

Thank You for every trial in my past and all

that You've taught me through each one. Thank You for the times You have set me alone and apart so that You could speak to my heart. Thank You, too, for the trials I face now and for whatever trials You have lovingly planned for my future. Give me grace to accept each one as a gift of love from You, as an invitation to closer, richer fellowship with You.

And give me grace to let Your enjoyable gifts lead me closer to You as the Giver, rather than letting them distract me or even become Your rivals.

In Jesus' name...

God's words of love for me today:
Psalms 31:14-16; 36:5-9; 69:13-16;
Isaiah 41:13; 1 Peter 4:12-13

Remember to record your answer to this question:
"What verse or phrase from these passages helps me most?"

My Path to Enlargement

One night I woke up and couldn't get back to sleep. After lying there awhile, I did what I often do in such predicaments: I went into my office next to our bedroom and read a few pages from daily devotional books by A. W. Tozer and Oswald Chambers. Something I read brought to my mind the thought, "Discouragement often precedes enlargement." Several friends and loved ones who were facing discouragement and worse came to mind. So I prayed that God, in His time, would use these difficulties to bring enlargement.

In my quiet time the next morning, Psalm 66:10-12 (NKJV) came to my attention:

For You, O God, have tested us;
You have refined us as silver is refined.
You brought us into the net;
You laid affliction on our backs.
You have caused men to ride over our heads;
We went through fire and through water;
But You brought us out to rich fulfillment.

Through this passage the Lord reminded me of how He works: He uses not only discouragement but also desperate situations to bring new release and enlargement into our lives—greater fulfillment and abundance and growth. The more desperate and impossible our situation, the more glory it can bring to God.

Think of Abraham as Romans 4:19 describes him—his body as good as dead. And think of Daniel's three friends, thrown into the blazing furnace (Daniel 3). Tough times, testings of faith—but great results! I found myself encouraged to believe this principle and pray accordingly.

Isn't such release and enlargement exactly what we want? In dealing with trials, I've found it helpful to have my true goals for my life clearly set and to keep them in my consciousness: to love God and know Him better, to be conformed to Christ's image, to glorify Him and do His will.

Then when I feel disappointed or distressed, the Lord can more quickly bring me back to this perspective: "This trial comes to help me reach my chosen goals even though it frustrates my surface desires. Therefore I welcome it."

Isn't it wonderful that we can count on One who is all-powerful and all-wise and who loves us perfectly? I often go back to the stanza by Frances Havergal:

> *Every joy or trial falleth from above,*
> *Traced upon our dial by the Sun of love.*
> *We may trust Him fully, all for us to do.*
> *They who trust Him wholly, find Him wholly true.*

So we can celebrate every trial because of God's ability to use it to make us more faithful, more like Christ. Our celebration can take the form of exuberance or simply a quiet purpose of heart. Either way, how appropriate it is to celebrate, in view of who God is, who we are in Christ, and what He is making of us by His transforming touch! When I fail to celebrate—as when I struggle with "too much to do"—I lose both spiritual joy and physical vitality.

My favorite praise word is *exult*. What a heart-expanding word! It's what the team and its loyal fans do when they win the national championship or the World Series or the

Super Bowl. If sports fans have reason to be elated, how much more do we! I like to think of exulting as lifting my heart above the frustrating, the pressing, the frightening, the sordid—lifting it up to the Lord with a sense of glad triumph.

In Romans 5 (NASB), Paul speaks of exulting not only in our God and our hope, but also exulting in our trials. Why can we exult in trials? Because of our God and our hope— our loving, sovereign, caring God and the glorious destiny He's preparing us for. "Whatever we may have to go through now is less than nothing compared with the magnificent future God has planned for us" (Romans 8:18, Phillips). So it's altogether reasonable to exult in our troubles—to "welcome them as friends!" as Phillips puts it in James 1:2-4.

Father, I love You. I praise and adore You for Your boundless love and wisdom. Thank You for Your perfect, loving design for my life, and for the way it includes both joys and trials. I rejoice that whatever happens in my life is so very small compared to the magnificent eternal future You have planned for me. And I thank You for revealing Your love to me in Your Word as, time and again, the Holy Spirit stirs my heart with the wonder of being loved by You.

Enable me in fresh ways to exult in You and Your love, and to exult in the hope (the happy certainty about the future) that You've given me through Christ. And Lord, remind me often to exult also in the testings You send, and in why You send them—to bring new release and enlargement into my life.

God's words of love for me today:
Psalms 31:7-8; 66:8-12; Romans 5:3-5;
Ephesians 2:4-7; James 1:2-5

He Is More Than Sunshine

It's easy to want our lives to be all beauty and no cost, all gain and no loss. When a difficulty mars the scene, we find ourselves focusing on our disappointment rather than treasuring life's delights. Job asked, "Shall we indeed accept good from God and not accept adversity?" (2:10, NASB). God wants us to receive both good and adversity with open hands and a trusting heart.

As I meditated on the birth of Christ one Christmas season in the late 1950s, the Lord gave me fresh insight about trials. He reminded me that the first Christmas, though beautiful, was costly. Oh, God gave special revelations and privileges, and He provided for and preserved Jesus, Mary, and Joseph in exciting ways. But in no sense did He coddle them. The cost included the arduous seven-day journey from Nazareth to Bethlehem, the far-from-glamorous birth-place, the hurried flight to Egypt to escape Herod. And for Jesus, much more:

He left the heavenly hills above
To die on Calvary's mountain,
Left the eternal springs of love
To taste earth's bitter fountain.

If our Father did not pamper His beloved Son, should we expect Him to pamper us? Jesus Himself assures us in John 16:33, "In this world you will have trouble [pressures, trials, tribulations, hardships, sorrows]. But take heart! I have overcome the world" (NIV). We can choose to take heart, to cheer up, and therefore to experience His peace in the midst of the pressures and costly trials. Or we can dissipate our energies through negative attitudes and pockets of inner resistance.

Often when my feelings cry, "Oh, if only life would get easier," a quotation from Phillips Brooks, an Episcopal bishop in the 1800s, motivates me to choose a different attitude—to open my arms wide and receive what God gives me to do, along with His sufficiency to accomplish it:

Do not pray for easier lives;
Pray to become stronger men.
Do not pray for tasks equal to your powers;
Pray for powers equal to your tasks.

Then your life shall be no miracle,
But you shall be a miracle.
Every day you shall wonder
At that which is wrought in you
By the grace of God.

Frequently my heart is touched by a prayer of George Matheson, the blind Scottish pastor who wrote "O Love That Wilt Not Let Me Go." Matheson has long been a model for me of being receptive and responsive to God in the midst of trials. He addresses his prayer to God as Spirit, who constantly desires fellowship with us. Here's the prayer. I trust it will mean as much to you as it has to me:

O Thou Divine Spirit, that in all events of life art
knocking at the door of my heart, help me respond to
Thee. I would take the events of my life as good and
perfect gifts from Thee; I would receive even the sor-
rows of life as disguised gifts from Thee. I would have

*my heart open at all times to receive—at morning,
noon, and night; in spring, and summer, and winter.
Whether Thou comest to me in sunshine or in rain, I
would take Thee into my heart joyfully. Thou art
Thyself more than the sunshine, Thou art Thyself
compensation for the rain; it is Thee and not Thy gifts
I crave; knock, and I shall open unto Thee. Amen.*

O God, my Reward and my Rewarder, I must know You. You Yourself are truly the one thing in life that I demand, the one and only thing I cannot live without. I choose to diligently seek You, to earnestly pursue my relationship with You. You are my first love. My goal is You—not the peace or joy or blessings You give, but You Yourself.

Lord, in the midst of my joys and my trials, work in me a constant responsiveness to You, a constant walk in the sunshine of Your love.

God's words of love for me today:
Numbers 6:24-26; Psalms 27:1; 43:3-5; 108:1-5;
Malachi 4:2

Everything About Him Says Something About Me

Perfect love—that's the way God's love is described in 1 John 4:18. And since His love is perfect, it cannot be improved. It will never become better, for it's already flawless and full and complete. God already loves us perfectly, so we never have to try to get Him to love us more!

His is the *only* perfect love. One verse in the Bible (1 John 3:1, Wuest) describes God's love as "exotic," as "foreign to the human heart." It is strikingly different, delightful, captivating. It's something extraordinary that's beyond our natural capacity to fully grasp. This means God's love is far better than any earthly love you'll ever find. Even your dearest friend or loved one cannot offer you love that is flawless, limitless, unmarred, and available around the clock every day of your life. God's love is the only perfect love.

There's a reason God's love is perfect: It is linked inseparably with everything He is. As I've thought about God through the years, I've been amazed by the wonderful blend of qualities we find in Him. I like to think of His strong side and also of His tender side. Most people don't have a good balance of strength and tenderness, but God does. In Him they blend and mingle together perfectly.

God's strong side is revealed in His power, majesty, holiness, glory, righteousness, and sovereignty. He is the supreme, almighty Ruler of the entire universe.

And His tender side is revealed in His warmth, graciousness, kindness, goodness, mercy, and understanding. As Ephesians 1:8 says in *The Living Bible,* "He has showered down upon us the richness of his grace—for how well he understands us and knows what is best for us at all times."

All these qualities—and scores more—are behind God's love. That's why we're not to pick and choose among His attributes, focusing on certain ones while ignoring others. All of God's attributes are intertwined, and they all undergird His personal, intimate, faithful love for you and me.

There's another good reason to ponder deeply all of

God's attributes: By doing so we learn more about ourselves. For not only does God give us clear, direct statements in His Word about who we are, but everything about *Him* reflects something about you and me as His children, His friends, His treasured possessions, His dwelling places who are one with Him in an intimate, inner union that will never end.

Therefore, as we explore God's love, we can more fully realize, "This means that I am a person who is loved with a perfect love." And as we learn more about God's infinite power, we can be assured, "I am secure and nothing can truly harm me, for He holds me safely in His almighty hand."

As I've studied Romans 15:4-5 in several versions, I've discovered that God is the God of perseverance and encouragement. These are His own personal attitudes. He will always persevere in relating to us and working in our lives, patiently enduring our ups and downs. He will never get discouraged and give up. And He is the source of perseverance and encouragement for us. He gives us perseverance to run the race that lies before us, and He encourages us through Christ and through the Scriptures. No wonder the psalmist said, "My flesh and my heart may fail, but God is the strength of my heart and my portion forever" (Psalm 73:26, NIV). God Himself is our inner strength.

Everything about *Him* reflects something about *me*.

Because of who our Lord is we can feel loved and secure, for we *are* loved and secure. These are facts, and God wants us to know them and to see ourselves in this light. He wants us to know Him, because everything we know about Him encourages us and gives us confidence, the ability to hold our heads high—not in pride, but in the light of His love.

We can find such excitement in exploring different truths about God revealed in the Bible because these truths enable us to appreciate His love more fully. They help us to look at Him in worship, praising and adoring Him. They also help us look to Him in dependence, putting our faith in Him. The clearer our understanding of what our God is like, the more we're able to trust Him and rest in the depths of His love.

My wonderful and glorious King, I bow in worship before You, rejoicing at the wonderful blend of attributes I find in You. How strong You are, yet how tender! Your majesty and glory and sovereign power are mingled so beautifully with Your warm love and goodness and mercy. I rest in the perfection of who You are and of how perfectly You love me.

And how I rejoice and rest in the gratifying

truth that everything about You reflects something about me. Remind me, Lord, when I'm impressed with a truth about You, to thank You for what this reflects about me. How privileged I am to be Yours!

I praise You for Your perfect love—love that is boundless, unchanging, and faithful, love that will endure forever. Love of every love the best! Thank You that Your love perfectly dovetails with all my needs and enriches me in countless ways every hour of every day. What a joy to know that I am someone who is loved with a perfect love!

God's words of love for me today:

1 Chronicles 29:11-12; Lamentations 3:19-26; Romans 11:33-36;
2 Corinthians 9:8; 1 John 4:18-19

He Is Altogether Desirable

One truth about God that deeply motivates me to explore His attributes is this: He is totally desirable. God is "the most winsome of all beings," as A. W. Tozer put it.

One place in Scripture where we can especially focus on God's winsomeness is Psalm 45, an allegory about a young woman chosen to be the bride of an excellent, most admirable King. The psalm extols a Person who infinitely surpasses any mere human, even the most magnificent earthly king. By highlighting the wonders of our heavenly King and Bridegroom, the psalmist seeks to draw us into a joyful surrender to Him.

If we really see what our Lord Jesus is like, we can't help but be captivated. Jesus manifested this winsomeness on earth. You remember, for example, how He came to Levi at his tax-collector's table and said, "Follow Me." Though despised by the Jews, Levi had a lucrative business and he probably walked in a rather wealthy social circle. He would be leaving a lot to follow Jesus. But there was something about this Person that drew him.

> *I heard Him call, "Come follow."*
> *That was all.*
> *My gold grew dim.*
> *My soul went after Him.*
> *I rose and followed. That was all.*
> *Who would not follow if they heard Him call?*
> —AUTHOR UNKNOWN

If we get a good look at Jesus, I believe we'll be moved to want to follow Him with all of our being. Even if we've already made the commitment to be His very own with no strings attached, we all still need to be folded more deeply into the will of God. Over time He keeps invading new territory in our lives to make us more totally His.

In verse 1 of Psalm 45 the psalmist tells us that his heart is bubbling up and overflowing with a beautiful theme as he addresses the King. Then in verse 2 he says to the King, "You are the most excellent of men." What does this mean? It means that our King "excels in manly traits and beauty" *(The NIV Study Bible).*

We know what it is to deeply admire someone. Imagine what would happen if you and I and all of our friends were each to choose the two people in our lives whom we most admired. Then imagine that we could take the single most outstanding character quality from each of them and transfer all those virtues into just one person. That person would be tremendous, don't you think? But he would still fall short of our wonderful Lord, for He is the most excellent of all human beings. Where they all leave off, He's still infinitely greater and better.

Jesus is indeed the bridegroom described by the bride in Song of Solomon 5. Using the most elaborate terms she can think of, she compares Him to the costliest things imaginable, such as gold and ivory and precious stones. Then in verse 16 she concludes, "He is altogether lovely" or, as the *Revised Standard Version* says, "altogether desirable."

This is the One who wants our love. He wants us to go to the Scriptures and discover how desirable He truly is. As we do this, something deep within us responds in worship.

Why? Because He meets our inborn need to adore someone without reservation, with no fear of finding ourselves disillusioned.

We read in Jeremiah 10:7, "For among all the wise men of the nations and in all their kingdoms, there is none like You" (NASB). If we compared with Christ all the wise and great men of the nations through all time, each one would fall immeasurably short of our glorious King. He is the most excellent of all who have ever lived.

You are altogether desirable, O Lord—in every way perfect and beautiful. I praise You for revealing Yourself in Your Word, so that I can behold Your beauty, delight in it, and let it fill my soul. Teach me to do this more and more.

You are my God, and I ask You to be in control of my activities and pursuits, of my commitments, of my relationships. I want to be Your child in Your place for me, doing Your will in whatever circumstances You see fit. I'm willing to wait until I'm with You in glory for the rewards You promise.

In faith and hope I focus my heart on You. I delight in You as my chief reward, for You are infinitely more excellent, more delightful, than anyone or anything in all the earth.

In Jesus' name…

God's words of love for me today:

Psalm 45:1-2; Isaiah 40:10-11; Jeremiah 10:6-7;

1 Timothy 1:17; Revelation 21:3-4

He Is My Champion

For tough times and difficult situations, I especially like to turn to verses 3 and 4 in Psalm 45. These again are words that the psalmist addresses to the King:

Gird your sword upon your side, O mighty one;
clothe yourself with splendor and majesty.
In your majesty ride forth victoriously
in behalf of truth, humility and righteousness;
let your right hand display awesome deeds. (NIV)

This is a favorite passage not only for prayer but also for worship and praise. It helps me mingle an attitude of praise with requests for victory, both for myself and others. And it tells us several things about what our Beloved is like.

For one thing, He's the mighty One. There is no one stronger. Don't we admire strength in a man, especially if the man is also caring and reliable? That's what we have in our Beloved. He is the most mighty One, and we're able to rely on Him in every way, in every time of need.

Another of my favorite passages on God's power is the prophet's cry to God in Jeremiah 32:17: "Ah, Lord GOD! Behold, You have made the heavens and the earth by Your great power and outstretched arm. There is nothing too hard for You" (NKJV). For One who created the whole universe, nothing is too complex or troublesome or demanding. All power in heaven and on earth is His.

Ten verses later, God answers Jeremiah and affirms His might. Here He mentions something else besides His ability to create the heavens and the earth. He says, "Behold, I am the LORD, *the God of all flesh.* Is there anything too hard for Me?" (NKJV).

It's as if He says, "Yes, I am the God who fashioned heaven and earth, and this shows My power. But I am also the God who is deeply interested in people. I'm the God of all mankind, able to control events, able to protect you and take care of you. I'm down here involved in people's lives, with all My limitless power."

That's what we need, isn't it? Limitless power coupled with limitless love and dedicated to helping us as His people, so that no problem needs to seem too big.

As Corrie ten Boom said, "There's no panic in heaven." God never presses the panic button. Moving on our behalf is easy for Him. And prayer releases His power. "Prayer is the slender nerve that moves the mighty hand of God."

As we've seen in Psalm 45:4, the writer prays to our awesome King with these words: "In your majesty ride forth victoriously in behalf of truth, humility and righteousness" (NIV). I like to use this in many situations that I—and others—face. I pray, "Lord, in this situation, in this life, ride forth victoriously. Defeat the enemy's evil purposes and bring about Your good and perfect will."

Often I need God to ride forth victoriously in my life because of an inner enemy that needs defeating—a fleshly attitude or desire—and He is more mighty than any inner enemy. Or I need Him to ride forth victoriously against some scheme or attack of Satan or into circumstances with which I cannot cope. Sometimes I simply pray, "You are my King, O God; command victories" (Psalm 44:4, NKJV).

We know that whenever the Lord rides forth, it's always to victory. He has never yet been defeated and never will be.

He is Victor. The very name Jesus means "Jehovah Savior, Jehovah Victor." He is Victor over every enemy. As Corrie ten Boom often said, "Jesus was Victor, Jesus is Victor, Jesus will be Victor—so don't wrestle, just nestle."

This is the kind of King we can call on. Prompted by His unfailing love and acting according to His infinite greatness, He will always answer us. We can utterly depend on His constancy—though His timing may differ from ours.

We have Someone to champion our cause. That Someone is our God of love—perfect love that is inseparably linked with perfect power and wisdom. He is the King of all the earth, the God who acts in behalf of the one who waits for Him. His eyes search the whole earth in order to strongly support those whose hearts are fully committed to Him (Isaiah 64:4; 2 Chronicles 16:9).

O Lord my Champion, I worship You as the most mighty One; nothing is too difficult for You. I worship You as the Victor, before whom every enemy must fall. I praise You for the limitless power You bring to bear on my problems and difficult situations. And I thank You that trials are the raw materials for Your victories.

You are truly my Champion, my ever-present Help in trouble. Ride forth victoriously, O Lord, in all that I face today. Defeat the enemy's evil purposes and bring about Your good and perfect will. Help me more and more to heartily lay hold of Your greatness.

In Jesus' name...

God's words of love for me today:
Deuteronomy 33:27, 29; Psalms 18:1-3,19; 45:3-5; Isaiah 64:4; Jeremiah 32:17; Romans 8:35-37

Remember to record your answer to this question:
"What verse or phrase from these passages helps me most?"

He Soars to My Help

The Lord is always with us, daily bearing the burden of our lives. As Psalm 46:1 says, He's an ever-present help in trouble, immediately available in tight places. But I also find it a blessing to think of Him in His high position of supreme authority, far above heaven and earth, far above all enemy powers. Then I pray that He, my mighty Champion, will "ride forth" from His vantage point, from His sure-to-win position, and work mightily.

Another psalm I love to soak in now and then is Psalm 68. Here David speaks of the Lord riding through the deserts and through the skies as if on a huge eagle or on a horse with wings. Why does He ride like this, in awesome power? He's speeding on His way to help us.

Time after time, Psalm 68:4 has helped me pray with confidence and praise to this One who rides forth on our behalf.

I especially like the way the early editions of the *New American Standard Bible* read:

> *Sing to God, sing praises to His name,*
> > *cast up a highway for Him who rides through*
> > *the deserts, whose name is the LORD, and exult*
> > *before Him.*

What a God we worship, so worthy of our praise, so heart-expanding as we exult before Him! Psalm 68 shows Him involved in the deserts of human experience, meeting the needs of the fatherless, the widows, the lonely, the prisoners, the parched, the poor. It shows Him meeting needs abundantly: "When you marched through the wasteland…you gave abundant showers, O God; you refreshed your weary inheritance" (68:7,9, NIV). The God we praise is deeply concerned about us and has committed Himself to care for us as we trust Him.

This psalm connects our praise with casting up a highway for our loving, mighty God who rides through deserts. A similar connection is found in Psalm 50:23 (NIV)—

> *He who sacrifices thank offerings honors Me,*
> > *and he prepares the way*
> > *so that I may show him the salvation of God.*

Through praise and thanksgiving we can help provide a highway that lets Him speed along unhindered to rescue and provide.

Because praise increases our faith as we pray, it opens the way for God to bring a multitude of benefits our way. These blessings, in turn, call forth fresh praise. And praise helps us fulfill the chief purpose to which God has called us: to glorify God and enjoy Him forever.

Don't you like the attitude of praise and trust exhibited by these psalmists? With them we can say, "Lord, You are a wonderful, majestic, powerful, gracious, caring God. We can count on You to win victories and to bless abundantly."

Lord, I worship You as God Most High, the great King over all the earth. You are the high and exalted One whose name is Holy, who inhabits eternity— who dwells far above and beyond us, unlimited by time and space!

I praise You as the One who rides—who soars—upon the highest heavens, who speeds through the skies in Your majesty to help us. You sweep down to the earth and ride through the deserts of our human experience, coming to the aid of the fatherless, the widows, the lonely, the prisoners, the poor, and the needy. You ride forth to help us when we recognize how destitute and helpless we are in ourselves to obey You, when we're burdened and need deliverance, when we dwell in a parched and thirsty land where there's no water.

And as You march through the wilderness, the earth quakes and the skies shake at Your presence, O God! And the heavens pour down rain—a plentiful rain that refreshes us, revives us, and meets our needs.

And our enemies flee before You. As smoke is blown away by the wind, You blow them away, scattering them, making them flee. At Your Presence, mountains of satanic opposition melt like wax before a fire.

You are the most mighty One, an awesome Warrior, splendid, majestic, triumphant—and loving! You are for us a God of victories! I exult before You and rejoice with gladness. And I pray that today You will ride forth and act on the requests I bring to You now....

God's words of love for me today:
Deuteronomy 33:26-27;
Psalms 33:18-22; 68:4-10; 94:18-19; 107:43

He Is Always
in Control

A few years ago I was in the garage unpacking one of the boxes we had sent from Singapore when we returned to the U.S. (It was another small, quick stab at a huge job that had begged for months to be done.) In one box I came across something a friend had made for us years earlier; she had beautifully embroidered a phrase from 1 Timothy 6:15 in the Phillips translation: "God is the blessed controller of all things."

I hung it just inside our bedroom door where I would see it often. Since then I've meditated on this verse time after time, situation after situation, by day and by night. I say to God, "You are *blessed*—warm and caring, generous, gracious. And You are *in control.* You are God Most High, and You work all things into a pattern for good for all who love You."

What a peace producer!

A number of years earlier, my husband, Warren, had seen this same quotation displayed in a home in India, and it had a similar impact on him. At the time he wrote the following:

> *This truth…has dominated my thinking and praying ever since I saw it, greatly strengthening my faith and praise. It has given me confidence and thankfulness for the way God orders events, influences, and chance contacts. It has also helped my attitudes and reactions toward those who, intentionally or not, inconvenience me, resist me, or make demands that seem unreasonable. This is a special cause for rejoicing because being gracious and patient is often hard for me, especially with the pressures of traveling in other cultures. What a rich encouragement the entire passage has become, reminding me that God is always in control, always seeking to bless us through whatever He sends or permits.*
>
> *"God, who is the blessed controller of all things, the king over all kings and the master of all masters,*

the only source of immortality, the one who lives in
unapproachable light.... To him be acknowledged all
honor and power forever, amen!"

(1 TIMOTHY 6:15-16, PHILLIPS)

God is always at the controls. Ephesians 1:11 says that He works all things after the counsel of His own will. *All things!* That circumstance in your life, which is causing you pain or dismay or confusion or worse, is not accidental. As someone has said, "With God nothing is accidental, nothing is incidental, and no experience is wasted." God allows certain painful experiences and uses them for His purposes. He is looking out for us, and He won't let anything happen to us that He can't use for our good, just as He has promised.

In Psalm 45:6 the inspired writer praises the King with these words: "Your throne, O God, is forever and ever" (NKJV). Our Beloved will never be dethroned. He will always be ruling over all; He will always be sovereign. And He's not just a king; He's the King of kings! So we need never fear.

That's why even now we can actively enjoy the fact that we're on the winning side, though it may not look like it in our world today or in our personal situation. Our King is ruling behind the scenes, never losing a battle for one of His own, as we count on Him in simple faith. Soon the day will come when His rule and His sovereignty will be obvious to all. Then everyone will see and recognize that He rules forever.

Verse 6 of Psalm 45 continues, "A scepter of justice will be the scepter of your kingdom" (NIV). His is a "scepter of righteousness" (NKJV). Because the golden scepter with which He rules is right and just, we can depend on Him never to make a mistake with our lives. We can count on His decrees and decisions to be always wise and always best.

The psalm continues, "You love righteousness and hate wickedness" (45:7, NIV). Our King is righteous through and through, and His love for us is altogether a righteous love. We need never suspect any ulterior motives in His dealings with us. He will never wrong us; He'll never lie to us; He'll never do anything we cannot admire. So we can give ourselves totally to loving Him and depending on Him. With all the corruption in the world in places high and low, we find few people we can depend on unreservedly. But God is totally dependable. There will never be any corruption in His government.

What a sense of peace this truth gives! God is so perfectly the kind of Ruler we need.

Loving Father, I exult in Your perfect sovereignty. "Your throne, O God, is forever and ever." I praise You as the Blessed Controller of all things everywhere—and of all things in my life. Thank You for the peace You give as I trust in Your wise control over all that has happened in my past, over everything I face today, and over all that the future will hold.

Now, Lord, continue to increase my capacity for seeking and knowing You. I plead with You to make me more thirsty for You.

I ask especially that I will hear Your voice of love morning by morning as I open Your Word and come to You. Through Your Holy Spirit, let the waters of Your love wash over me. Let me swim in the truth of Your loving, sovereign control. And change my life as a result.

In Jesus' name...

God's words of love for me today:
Psalms 103:19; 115:1-3; Isaiah 46:9-11;
Jeremiah 29:11-13; 1 Timothy 6:14-17

His Perfect Faithfulness to Me

God's perfect love is inseparable from His perfect faithfulness.

Again and again the psalmists link God's love with His faithfulness (or, as the *King James Version* says, His truth). For example, Psalm 36:5 says, "Your love, O LORD, reaches to the heavens, your faithfulness to the skies" (NIV). The Lord's faithfulness exceeds by far any human faithfulness.

The Lord is always faithful and true—true to His Word, true to His character, true to each of His loved ones. He is never unfaithful, never untrue. He is faithful to bless us and faithful to chasten us: "In faithfulness you have afflicted me" (Psalm 119:75, NIV); "Before I was afflicted I went astray, but now I obey your word" (119:67, NIV).

God is faithful to sanctify us completely, keeping our spirit, soul, and body sound and blameless until Christ returns (1 Thessalonians 5:23-24). He is faithful to forgive us as soon as we confess our sins (1 John 1:9). His forgiveness is always glad and immediate, never grudging or delayed. He never says, "Well, I'll wait and see how much better you do." He is faithful to fulfill all His promises: Not one single word of all His good promises has ever failed (1 Kings 8:56). And He promises to love us forever. Nothing will ever separate us from His love (Romans 8:38-39).

One of my favorite Scriptures on the Lord's faithfulness is Lamentations 3:21-24. Jeremiah had been going through prolonged and traumatic trials; finally all his hopes had been dashed. After recounting his bitter afflictions, he says in verse 21, "This I call to mind, and therefore I have hope" (RSV). What did he remember that gave him hope in a hopeless situation? He tells us in verses 22-24: "The steadfast love of the LORD never ceases, his mercies never come to an end; they are new every morning; great is thy faithfulness. 'The LORD is my portion,' says my soul, 'therefore I will hope in Him'" (RSV).

The writer of Psalm 42 also turned his mind to God and His constant love. The psalmist was in exile—mourning, oppressed, weeping day and night. His heart was disquieted, discouraged, downcast.

His solution? See verse 6 (NIV), "O my God, my soul is cast down within me; therefore I will remember You." And what did he remember? The Lord's constant and faithful love: "The LORD will command His lovingkindness in the daytime, and in the night His song shall be with me" (verse 8, NKJV).

I have found that, no matter how discouraging or hopeless or pressing my situation may be, there's some truth about God that can encourage me, give me hope, and bring me through triumphantly—when I remember Him, calling to mind what He is like. When I turn my mind and heart to Him, focusing on who He is according to His Word, He is faithful to restore my soul. He repairs and heals my inner person. He refreshes me as water refreshes a dry and wilted plant.

Often through the years, the Lord has used the following lyrics by Katharina von Schlegel to quiet and reassure my soul:

> *Be still, my soul: the Lord is on thy side;*
> *Bear patiently the cross of grief or pain;*

Leave to thy God to order and provide;
In every change He faithful will remain.
Be still, my soul: thy best, thy heavenly Friend
Through thorny ways leads to a joyful end.

O my God and Father, Your love reaches to the heavens. It is too high and wonderful for my mind to grasp, but my heart rejoices and rests in it.

And again I celebrate with wonder the truth that Your love is a faithful love that never changes. How grateful I am for the steady overflow of Your love to me even though You know so well all that is worst about me.

I especially want to thank You for loving me even when I've been disobedient or rebellious toward You. How incredible is Your faithfulness to our relationship, Your loyalty and commitment to it! How it relieves my heart to remember that You have never turned away from me, and never will. You'll never let anything separate me from Your love!

God's words of love for me today:
Deuteronomy 7:6,9; 32:3-4; Hebrews 10:23;
Romans 8:38-39; Revelation 1:4-5; 3:14

His Lovingkindness Surrounds Me

Look with me at a delightful word, one of the best terms in Scripture for helping us understand God's perfect love.

One year I did a study, largely in the Psalms, on the Lord's *lovingkindness*. The *New American Standard Bible* uses this expression for an amazingly rich Old Testament word. Other translations render this word as "mercies," "steadfast love," "covenant love," "unfailing love," "kindness," or simply "love."

It's a tender word, showing the compassionate side of the Lord as He is actively involved with us, bestowing on us a multitude of lovingkindnesses. It is also a strong word, for embedded in its meaning is the concept of durability.

The most-used sentence of praise in the Bible reinforces this: "His lovingkindness endures forever."

Through my study, I discovered that God's lovingkindness is good, abundant, marvelous, precious, and better than life. It extends to the heavens, and the earth is full of it. It is from everlasting, and it will be built up forever. It is mine for all the days of my life and for all eternity. The Lord blesses with lovingkindness those who trust Him, who fear (revere) Him, who call upon Him.

Lovingkindness follows us, surrounds us, and crowns us. By it we enter the Lord's house, by it we expect answers to prayer, and through it we will stand unshaken, for it will hold us up when our feet slip. It satisfies us and is the one unfailing basis for rejoicing and being glad all our days. Lovingkindness is infused into all God is and into all He does (as you can see in Psalm 136).

The Lord wants me to pray about experiencing His lovingkindness, to rejoice in it, and to give thanks for it. He wants me to trust His lovingkindness and to hope in it, expecting Him to be loving and kind. He wants me to speak of it, to declare it to others.

Psalm 103:4 speaks of the Lord's "lovingkindness and tender mercies" (NKJV). This takes me back to Luke 1:78, which reminds us of "the tender mercy of our God, with which the Sunrise from on high" has visited us (NASB). Indeed, the Light from heaven, our Lord Jesus Christ who lived and died for us, was the supreme demonstration of God's lovingkindness.

Psalm 32:10 says, "He who trusts in the LORD, lovingkindness shall surround him" (NASB). Just think of His tender love encircling each of us, blessing and protecting us on all sides! This reminds me of a song that says, "I'm overshadowed by His mighty love"—but His love is not merely above me but also all around me like fresh air and warm sunshine.

Then in Psalm 52:1 we read, "The lovingkindness of God endures all day long" (NASB). It never lessens or wears thin as the day wears on, as our human love and kindness often do. All day, every day, it flows from His heart and envelops us as He constantly cares for us. And so God's perfect love fulfills every ideal that the human race has ever searched for in a relationship. As the godly Shirley Rice put it, "Once you've been loved by God, you are loved completely, and you do not need to grasp anymore."

No wonder the psalmist said in 59:16, "I shall joyfully sing of Your lovingkindness in the morning" (NASB). This joyful singing in the morning can result from praying as the psalmist did in 143:8, "Cause me to hear Your lovingkindness in the morning, for in You do I trust" (NKJV). What a good way to start the day: listening to God's lovingkindness and singing about it! This brings pleasure to God. "His joy is in those who reverence him, those who expect him to be loving and kind" (Psalm 147:11, TLB).

I'm also reminded of Psalm 36:7-9 (NIV):

How priceless is your unfailing love!
Both high and low among men
    find refuge in the shadow of your wings.
They feast on the abundance of your house;
    you give them drink from your river of delights.
For with you is the fountain of life.

The shelter of His wings offers not only protection but also delightful, refreshing living water and rich provision from His vast reserves.

Our hidden relationship with God connects us with an abundant flow of lovingkindness and life, both for us and for others through us.

Thank You, Lord God, for Your lovingkindness that surrounds me and overshadows me. Your

lovingkindness is better than life itself. How I rejoice that Your love endures forever—and that it
continues all day long, never wearing thin as our
human love so often does.

I'm especially grateful that Your tender mercy
moved You to send the Sunrise from on high and
that He came to shine on those who sat in darkness
and to guide our feet into the way of peace.

So I worship and praise You, for "there is none
like You, O Lord." Today, in new ways, in the midst
of joys and trials, display Your love and power to me
and through me to others.

Meanwhile I rest in the fact that I am loved so
completely and never again need to grasp for love
from those around me.

In Jesus' name…

God's words of love for me today:
Psalms 32:10-11; 59:16-17; 86:15-17;
136:1-9,26; 143:8-10

What Is He to Me?

We've been considering many of God's attributes and what they mean for us, His children. We have seen how awesome and adequate He is: altogether desirable, perfect in power and greatness, our Champion, the Blessed Controller of all things, perfectly faithful, surrounding us with lovingkindness.

Now the question is, *What is God to me day by day, moment by moment?*

The most important truth for my life is that God wants me to know Him intimately, personally. Yes, He wants me to know the concepts about Him that He has given us in His Word. But He wants me to take each of those truths and allow Him to *be that to me* in my personal experience. If we want to be realists, if we want to live realistically, we must know who God is and let Him be that for us.

So often there can be a sort of psychological distance between us and God. We can know and say, "God is my heavenly Father, He is a refuge in the storms of life, He is the source of deepest satisfaction"—but do these truths really mean much to us? Is our knowledge largely mental knowledge? After all, it's possible to recognize these truths but not experience them.

But God wants us to see ourselves linked with Him in every aspect of our lives. He wants to reveal Himself personally to us through the Bible so that we can, with our whole heart, respond to Him and say, *"My* Father, *my* Refuge, *my* Satisfaction." I've found through the years that this is what happens as we become more and more aware of what He wants to be to us.

To really know God means that we see what He wants to be in relationship to us and then, more and more in the experiences of daily life, *let* Him be that to us—*count on Him to be that.*

I have found Psalm 31 very helpful in this. In verse 2 David prays, "Be my rock of refuge, a strong fortress to save me" (NIV). Then in verse 3 he says, "Since you are my rock and my fortress...." At first I thought this sounded like double-talk: Be to me a rock because You are my rock. Then I realized that David is saying, "I have chosen You to be my rock; now be that for me in my situation right now. Be to me now what You are." Isn't that great?

Be to me what You are. You are my best love—be that to me now, for I need that today. You are the water of life—be that to me at this time, because my soul is thirsty.

Here's where praise comes in. We turn our eyes to what He is and give Him thanks and praise. Then our experience begins to line up with these truths, and He becomes more wondrously real to us.

We can keep running to Him, saying,

Be my Strength and my Redeemer…my Sun and my Shield…my Joy…my Counselor…my King…my loving Friend.

Oh, there are so many wonderful aspects of our God! We could devote many pages to listing them, and we still wouldn't begin to exhaust the wonders of who He is.

This is one of the most beautiful aspects of getting to know God better and letting our relationship with Him grip us in a new way. We find out what He is and then accept in our heart that He's that *to me!* Then we can say with ever-growing delight, "You are my good Shepherd, my Beloved, my Bridegroom, my Father."

Lord, it is so encouraging to reflect on how seriously You want me to take You and Your love, and how personally. So I choose to see myself through Your own all-knowing and all-loving eyes.

Open the eyes of my heart to take in new facets of Your relationship with me, and give me grace to count on them with growing constancy. In a deeper, richer way than ever before, be to me what You are.

God's words of love for me today:
Psalm 31:1-3; John 6:35; 8:12; 14:6; 15:5

Remember to record your answer to this question:
"What verse or phrase from these passages helps me most?"

Why He Loves Me

God loves us "just because." His love defies human logic. It doesn't make sense. Our human minds cannot figure it out. How could this holy God, Creator and Ruler of all things, have such deep love for us, tiny specks in a vast universe, who fall short of even our own ideals?

And yet there *are* reasons He loves us. I think of at least two. First, God loves us because He *is* love. It's His nature to love.

Second, God loves us because He made us. Sin has destroyed some of the beauty of His design that He must now work to restore; but He made each of us with great skill, and we have unique value to Him as His special workmanship— one of His originals.

Because He made us for Himself, in His image, we have the potential of intimate relationship with Him, and that intimacy is extremely important to Him. He highly prizes us and wants us for Himself, knowing what a love relationship with Him can mean to us—and to Him—in this life.

God also loves us for what He knows we'll become for all eternity—beautiful, living works of art, bringing glory and pleasure to Him as He continues to lavish His riches on us. He eagerly awaits the delights in store for Him and us when we dwell with Him forever in joyful, unbroken fellowship.

We read in Deuteronomy 7:7 and 10:15 that God set His love upon His people—He "fastened" it upon them, as *The Berkeley Version* says. I like that. There's a gentle but unyielding persistence about the love of God, a tenacious tenderness toward each person who has responded to Him. He loves us and holds on to us and won't let us go.

Now if someone who was not generous and loving were to fasten himself onto you, it could make you uncomfortable. But God is incredibly generous and loving, and His tenacity makes you secure.

I realize that much of what I share in these thirty-one days is not really new to you. But I know that, as we look at God anew, as we focus our gaze on Him, our knowledge of familiar truths about Him becomes truer and deeper.

What's more, if we then let our hearts praise and adore

and worship Him, something will happen deep in our emotional nature. It's like the feeling that comes when you pause to fully appreciate a sunset, when its beauty overwhelms you and your heart rises in admiration. A similar response can arise when we take a closer look at God. And this sense of admiration is important both to Him and to our own well-being.

We know we've begun to go deep into God's love when we can say to Him the words David prayed in Psalm 63:3—"Your love is better than life" (NIV). Wouldn't you rather give up life in this world than to be separated from the love of God?

I like the way two verses in Song of Songs portray God's love: "Your love is more delightful than wine" (1:2), and "We will praise your love more than wine" (1:4, both NIV). In the Scriptures wine is often a symbol of joy. It offers release from inhibitions—sometimes too much!—and relief from fears and anxieties. But anything wine can do for a person, God's love can do better—and without the side effects. You can take in all you want of His love without worrying about a headache the next morning. His love is better—and we find this to be so true when we simply drink of His love as often as we need it.

God's love *is* better than life.

Lord God, I praise You that You *are* love. I cannot fully comprehend Your reasons for loving me; yet I thank You that the perfect reasons are there in Your nature and in Your heart, and always will be.

Thank You for loving me eternally, for fastening Your love upon me before the foundation of the world. Thank You for the Holy Spirit, Your gracious gift to me, who is eager to pour out Your love in my heart more and more.

I pray that in new ways day by day, month by month, I'll be to You what You long for, as I let You and Your love be to me what I need.

God's words of love for me today:
Deuteronomy 7:7-9; 10:14-21;
Psalms 62:11-12; 130:7; 145:8-13,17-20

From Everlasting to Everlasting, He Loves Me

In the midst of my failures and struggles when I feel so undeserving, I never have to think, *Oh dear, does God still love me?* He never started loving me in the first place because I deserve it. He just loves me. His love for each of us is never rooted in our worthiness, but rather in His own nature.

"The lovingkindness of the LORD is from everlasting to everlasting on those who fear Him" (Psalm 103:17, NASB). *From everlasting to everlasting.* That's a long time, isn't it?

From everlasting, way back before I existed, God loved me. Long before I was born He looked ahead and fastened His affection upon me. His love for me began in His foreknowledge of me. That means He doesn't love me because I earned it, for when He decided to love me I did not even exist. God's love is not mine because I merit it, for He fastened His love upon me before I ever did one thing good or bad, before I ever merited anything.

God is saying to us, "It's not because you've earned it or worked so hard for it that I have loved you. And I don't continue loving you because you manage to maintain a high enough standard in my eyes. No, I simply made a permanent choice to love you."

And that choice will never change. God has loved me *from* everlasting and will love me *to* everlasting. His love for me—and for you—will never end. It's a lifelong, eternity-long relationship, now and forever available to meet our every need as we seek to know Him better.

God has always known all things. Before we were born He already knew the worst about us, and nothing that happens now can surprise or disillusion Him. He has never had any illusions about anyone or anything. He doesn't suddenly discover some truth about one of us and think, "Oh, why did I ever choose to love him or her?"

I like what J. I. Packer says in *Knowing God:* "God's love to me is utterly realistic, based at every point on the prior knowledge of the worst about me, so that no discovery now

can disillusion Him about me in the way I am so often disillusioned about myself, and quench His determination to
bless me."

In Isaiah 54:10, God says, "For the mountains may be
removed and the hills may shake, but My lovingkindness
will not be removed from you, and My covenant of peace
will not be shaken" (NASB). His lovingkindness is an unshakable love that will always be mine. This truth makes me
feel secure; it also makes me want to love Him in return.

The Berkeley Version of the Psalms speaks of His love as a
"covenant love." The One who cannot lie and cannot
change has made a covenant—a binding, unbreakable
agreement—to love us. He has given us His word that He'll
always continue to love us; He has committed Himself to
doing so.

And He will never change His mind. God will never di-
vorce us, because He's given His promise and He cannot
break His word. It's an attitude and commitment that God
has freely chosen for Himself, and He will never, in any way,
go back on it.

Deuteronomy 7:7-9 tells exciting truths about God's
love for His people Israel. If we belong to the Lord, we are
now His people through the new, everlasting covenant He
has made with us in Christ. So we can claim these truths in

an even greater way than the Israelites of old could. In this passage we read that God set His love upon His people and chose them, but not because of their greatness. In fact He reminds them that they were the least of the nations. He chose them to be His valued possession, His special treasure, simply because of His love and His promises. Likewise God has chosen us simply because He loves us, and He has made promises that guarantee that love for all time and eternity.

Hebrews 13:8 says that Jesus Christ is the same yesterday and today and forever. When Jesus walked on the earth, He was a living demonstration of God's love for us. Remember the love Jesus exhibited, the intimate involvement He sought with people, the intense concern and care He showed in meeting people's needs? He is the same today. His love is rooted in His nature, and it will never change. It is everlasting and will never end (Jeremiah 31:3).

Dear Lord, what a comfort it is to know that You will never withdraw Your love for me, that You will love me forever.

I celebrate with glad wonder the truth that Your love never changes. How grateful I am for its steady flow from Your heart to mine, even though You know all that is worst about me—and even though

I disobey You. How my heart rejoices to remember that You will never turn away from me!

Thank You that both in this life and throughout all eternity I will continue to discover more and more of Your love—and that, because Your love is limitless, I will never stop experiencing it in fresh and different ways.

I pray, Lord, that day by day You will make Yourself and Your love a living, bright reality to me. And do the same for those whose names I bring before You now....

God's words of love for me today:
Psalms 23:6; 25:4-7; 40:11; 103:13-18;
Isaiah 54:10

He Cannot Let Me Go

Even when I'm letting something else be more important to me than God, God is still loving me. Even when He must discipline me, He says, "I won't go one bit farther than I have to for your good, and I will never cut you off from My love. My heart would never allow it." He recoils at the very thought of ever withdrawing His love from us.

In the book of Hosea we see this unchanging love of God in an especially beautiful way. There God declared that He still loved His people "though they turn to other gods" (3:1, NIV). Through the prophet Hosea's message the Lord shows how constant His love for His people is, even when they spurn Him and persist in rebelling against Him.

I once came across a new version of Hosea in a booklet

called *Just as Now,* where God speaks these words to His people in Hosea 11:8—"I cannot just cut you off. My heart recoils within me. How can I let you go?" The *Good News Bible* says, "How can I abandon you? My heart will not let me do it! My love for you is too strong." And the *New Living Translation* puts it this way, "Oh, how can I give you up, Israel? How can I let you go? My heart is torn within me, and my compassion overflows."

These words reflect God's attitude toward the Israelites even though they had persistently rebelled against Him. Over the centuries God had patiently sent them warnings, but so often His people refused to listen. Finally He had to send severe chastening. They needed it, and He gave it. But even that chastening was evidence of His love, just as it is in our lives. Throughout it all His attitude was still, "How can I let you go?" He cannot give us up. He cannot abandon us. His love for us is too strong.

How that relieves my heart!

The Wuest expanded translation of 1 John 3:1 reads, "Behold what exotic love the Father has permanently bestowed upon us." His love is something bestowed, something He has given us—not because we could ever deserve it, but simply because we said yes to Him. By that simple, believing consent we were born into His family and are now called His children. We are and forever will be His children, because His love is unchanging and eternal, permanently bestowed. What joy is ours as we come to understand this truth more deeply!

The Lord wants us to find great joy in the human loves He brings into our lives. But these loves may not be lifelong, nor do they in any way measure up to His love. Our deepest and most satisfying love will always be our Father's love, and we can count on it for all our life on earth and for all eternity.

Psalm 73:26 (NIV) begins, "My flesh and my heart may fail"—yes, this will happen to us in different ways all through life. Our bodies and souls may grow weak, may waste away, may droop like a wilted flower. And worse than that, we may inwardly and outwardly fail to trust and obey the Lord. But we can come right back to Him, confess how we have failed, and absorb His love anew. Then we can personalize the last part of this verse, saying with the psalmist,

Lord, You are the strength of my heart, the source of my stability; and You are my chosen portion forever.

"You remain the same," David says to God in Psalm 102:27, "and your years will never end" (NIV). Because God remains constantly and forever the same, we can say also about His love,

> *Your love will never end. You will always have*
> *the same love for me, the same heart-involvement*
> *with me!*

God's love holds on—and this perfect, permanent love gives us real stability. Many times I've told Him, "Lord, that's the kind of love I need—love that never fluctuates, never falters, never fails. If You didn't have that kind of love, surely You would have given up on me long ago!"

Thank You, Lord, for the hope and encouragement that are mine because I can always keep coming back to the wonderful truth: You will never abandon me, You will never let me go. Thank You that Your love for me is an enduring gift, permanently bestowed.

I choose also to thank You for the trials and discipline You bring my way because Your love is tough. Thank You for holding on to me and not holding back, and thank You for continuing Your tender care even when You're putting me through refining fires. In the midst of my trials—and my joys—make me more aware of You and Your love than of any visible things in my life. Do this today—and increasingly as the days go by.

In Jesus' name...

God's words of love for me today:
Psalm 73:23-24; Hosea 3:1; 11:8-9;
John 10:27-30; Philippians 3:12-14

His Love for Me Is Limitless

God's love is beyond words. The words we use only hint at what it is like, giving us glimpses of how wonderful it is. Only the Holy Spirit can illuminate these words in our hearts, bringing us into a greater experience of God's wondrous love.

God's love is incalculably great. His love is abounding, vast, infinite. His love has no limits, no boundaries. In both duration and extent it is limitless. We'll never be able to get out of it or away from it or beyond it.

In Ephesians 3:16-19, Paul speaks of how the Spirit within us strengthens us so that in fuller measure we can have Christ dwelling within us. Then he says, "I pray…that your life will be strong in love and be built on love" (NCV).

He goes on to pray that we will know through actual experience the greatness of Christ's love, that we will understand more fully its boundless dimensions—how wide and long and high and deep it is. Yet it will always be far greater than any of us will fully know.

Though we can never fully grasp with our minds how immense God's love is, to a wonderful degree we can experience it in our hearts. One poet, realizing how needy and undesirable he was in himself, how undeserving of such love, wrote these words:

How Thou couldst love me as I am
and be the God Thou art,
is darkness to my intellect
but sunshine to my heart.

God's love can warm our hearts even though it is so great we will never know and experience it in all its fullness. Yet we can press on to know it more fully.

God's love is limitless. It reaches out to each person on earth and reaches to me, whatever my attitude or situation. There are no bounds to the encouragement and hope and strength it can give us. Once in Singapore I found myself under unusual pressure while Warren was gone for almost a month. Situations arose that were difficult for me to cope with, especially without his objective counsel. In those stressful weeks the Lord deeply ministered to me through 2 Thessalonians 2:16-17: "Now may our Lord Jesus Christ Himself and God our Father, who has loved us and given us unending encouragement and unfailing hope by grace, comfort and strengthen your hearts in every good thing you say or do" (NASB and Phillips). How it warmed and quieted my heart to know that both the Lord Jesus Himself and my heavenly Father were eager to encourage and strengthen me in all that I needed to say and do!

These verses show God's personal, loving touch: encouragement and hope that never fail because they are by grace, not based on my deserving. My heart—and yours—may often fail and our resources prove to be inadequate. But the Lord Himself, who loves us, is always ready to inspire us with courage and confidence.

In Psalm 103:11, David says that "as high as the heavens are above the earth, so great is his love for those who fear him" (NIV). What a wonderful picture this is of God's overflowing, limitless, ever-present love. His love is as vast as the universe. We can never exhaust it, but we can fail to receive and enjoy it.

The Lord does not parcel out little dabs of love—"Well,

you've been a good child today, so I'll love you a little bit." No, His love flows freely. It overflows, coming to us in abundance. We read in Romans 5:5 that God's love has been poured out in our hearts by the Holy Spirit. It "floods our hearts," as James Moffatt translates it. God offers His love in a tremendous outpouring—not in skimpy measure, but rather in a flood, an inundation.

And He has put right within us the supplier of this abounding love—the Holy Spirit—so that His love can be poured out abundantly throughout our whole being. We don't have to settle for trivial little spoonfuls of His love. We can experience vastly more of it than we do now, if we truly want to—if we open ourselves to Him and His Word, seeking and trusting, yielding and asking for what we need.

Perhaps there's no fuller statement of how great God's love is than John 3:16: "God *so* loved the world...." God's love is *so* intense, *so* great, *so* deep. He loves us so much that He gave His Son, submitting Him to unimaginable, unprecedented agony for our sake. This is how God so loves us and every person on earth.

His love is "broader than the measure of man's mind," as the hymn says. No man's mind is great enough to fully grasp God's love. I've often ended letters to my children with the line, "I love you more than you know." And God loves us far more than we know and far more than we'll ever know. His love is so great that we'll never completely comprehend it.

This means there's always more about God's love for us to discover and enjoy.

The vastness of God's love also means we can always count on His love. It's always big enough to meet the deepest needs of our heart. Even in the best of earthly relationships, human love will not and cannot always be what we'd like it to be. In our own marriage, Warren's love wears thin once in a while and so does mine. But God's never does. As A. W. Tozer said in *The Pursuit of God,* "How completely satisfying to turn from our limitations to a God who has none."

Yours, O Lord, is the kingdom and the power and the glory. You are majestic and holy and filled with boundless love. You alone are worthy of all honor.

Thank You for surrounding me now and forever with Your limitless love, so incalculably great! Thank You that You are love, perfect and unfailing love—my only real home, my dwelling place, my shelter and shield, and my eternal resting place.

Lord, day by day give me a deeper and richer understanding of Your truth about me as Your loved one, a growing awareness of the unceasing favor and lovingkindness with which You view me. And as the earth receives the sunshine and the rain, grant me a growing constancy in simply absorbing Your love.

God's words of love for me today:
Psalms 86:5,12-13; 118:1-4; Romans 5:6-8;
Ephesians 3:16-19; 2 Thessalonians 2:16-17

Remember to record your answer to this question:
"What verse or phrase from these passages helps me most?"

Why I Qualify for His Love

God's love is linked inseparably with His grace, His attitude of unmerited favor toward us. Grace is the basis on which He first chose us in His love, and His overflowing grace is the basis on which He continues to lavish His love upon us.

We read in the Wuest translation of Romans 5:20 that where sin abounded, "grace superabounded with more added to that." There are no words to adequately convey the abundance of God's grace—of His special favor, His undeserved kindness.

God's love is so great that no sin is too great for Him to forgive. We can always approach His throne of grace and receive forgiveness, whether for an obvious, even repulsive sin or for any of the mass of little failures that get us down and prompt us to think, *Oh, do I have to confess that again?* God's love is all grace—just as I am, I come.

One initial condition, and one alone, is necessary for us to enjoy His love. We've met that condition if we have simply opened our lives to Jesus—if we have made the choice and prayed, "Yes, come in and be my Lord and Savior. You died for me, and I receive You into my life." At that point we're linked in a permanent personal relationship with God through His never-deserved, never-ending love.

In Ephesians 2:13, J. B. Phillips says that in Christ Jesus we are "inside the circle of God's love." We were outside that circle before, shutting ourselves off from our God of love. But we stepped inside by responding to Him in humble faith, admitting our sinfulness and opening ourselves up to experience His love.

In no way do we ever need to try to earn God's love; He loves us—period. The flow of His love for us never stops. His love always shines forth undimmed.

But our response to God's love determines whether it gets through to us. We can pull the blinds—or we can open them. We choose what we'll let ourselves be filled with, and God respects our choice. He does not force His love on us. But at all times His love flows and shines—perfect, unwavering, overflowing—always available to meet our needs.

We see this unchanging flow of God's love portrayed in the story of the prodigal son in Luke 15. The father was waiting for the son to end his rebellion and return home. And when he saw his son coming, he didn't have to think twice about responding with fervent love. The flow of his love had never lessened, though the son had strayed to a far country and into a sinful, depraved lifestyle.

All of us need this grace. All of us have to confess sin. The fact is, we *are* sinners—not we *were* sinners. We are forgiven sinners, and sin is no longer part of our core identity. But we still sin. The Lord gives us victory over certain sins and enables us to grow in holiness. But we still fall short of perfect holiness. As we mature through the years we see shortcomings and areas of neglect in our lives that we didn't recognize earlier. We always need God's undeserved forgiveness.

So often, when we feel we're doing well (if we've been victorious and had our quiet time every day and learned Bible verses and been nice to our family and our neighbors), then we think, *God surely loves me today.* Then we drop into those low times when we're sure there's no way He could love us now. So at the very point where we need His love most, we don't even dare go before Him to seek and experience it. We forget that He has always loved us even when we had absolutely no use for Him at all. And He will always love us—just because.

What qualifies us to receive God's love? We qualify simply because we need it. I'm reminded of C. S. Lewis's words: "Our whole being, by its very nature, is one vast need; incomplete, preparatory, empty yet cluttered, crying out to Him who can untie things that are now knotted together and tie up things that are still dangling loose."

David understood this. Psalm 40 reveals his honest heart as it portrays the kind of person God thinks about and demonstrates His lovingkindness to. David knew what it was to be in a slimy pit, in the mud and the mire. He cried out,

> *Do not withhold Your tender mercies from me, O LORD;*
> *Let Your lovingkindness and Your truth continually pre-*
> *serve me....*
> *My iniquities have overtaken me, so that I am not able to*
> *look up;*
> *They are more than the hairs of my head;*
> *Therefore my heart fails me....*
> *I am poor and needy;*
> *Yet the LORD thinks upon me.*
>
> (40:11,12,17, NKJV)

To the person who has desperate needs and is willing to admit them, God is eager to show His abundant love.

Do you qualify? I know I do. I qualify because I have needs—desperate needs. And God has made me willing to admit them and let Him meet them. When I fail to recognize how needy I am, He graciously works to remind me (at times in painful ways). And He renews my willingness to say, "Lord, I'm so messed up, so needy, so unable to obey You and to handle life in my own strength. So I bring my deep needs to You."

We qualify for the benefits of God's love because we are needy.

Father, I confess that I desperately need Your love, and always will. Thank You for the many ways You have met this need, for the many times You have flooded my heart with the reality of Your loving presence.

Lord, I acknowledge that You and You alone are the answer to all my needs. How I praise You that You are available to meet them so lavishly and generously with Your own fullness! I have no reason ever to turn elsewhere!

I exult in the grace You have lavished upon me

in delivering me from sin and death, welcoming me into Your inner circle of love, and drawing me into growing intimacy with You. I rejoice that I will enjoy this intimacy throughout all the future—that ours is a lifelong relationship that will last through all eternity.

Thank You especially, Lord, for Your grace in accepting me in spite of my imperfect life and service. This motivates me to want to serve You more. Give me grace to obey You and serve You in ways that will bring You increasing pleasure.

You are worthy, O Lord, worthy of my all and my best.

In Jesus' name…

God's words of love for me today:
Psalms 40:12,17; 109:21-22,30-31; 130:3-4;
Luke 15:11-24; 1 Corinthians 15:10

His Love for Me
Is Lavish

God delights to do the things that delight us, and so He gives to us lavishly.

In his book *Forever Triumphant,* F. J. Huegel put it like this: "When God gives, it is always in a multiplied fashion, something akin to the unnumbered millions of shining worlds in the boundless firmament of heaven." God certainly didn't have to put so many stars in the sky, but isn't it just like Him to fill our night skies with so much beauty for us to appreciate and admire with delight and awe?

He is not a stingy God.

Of course His intention is not to make us all rich materially. In His life on earth Jesus had few earthly possessions, but He was rich in all that truly mattered. And in leaving behind the riches of heaven as He came to this earth, His purpose was to share with us His true and eternal treasures: "For you know the grace of our Lord Jesus Christ, that though he was rich, yet for your sakes he became poor, so that you through his poverty might become rich" (2 Corinthians 8:9, NIV).

As part of these riches God has already made available to us everything we need here on earth for a full spiritual life and a satisfying emotional life: "His divine power has given us everything we need for life and godliness through our knowledge of him who called us by his own glory and goodness" (2 Peter 1:3, NIV). "Everything we need for life and godliness" is ours to enjoy as we seek to know God better.

And as He works in our lives to encourage and strengthen us, to develop and train us, even in this He is ultra-generous. He does *more* than we would expect Him to.

This has been an important lesson for me, because in my early teens I had a wrong concept of God. I was afraid of missing out on real happiness if I turned my life over to Him. So I held on to my life in fear. But as I became more and more miserable trying to work out my own wonderful plans, I finally told God He could do anything He pleased with my life. For the first time I began finding satisfaction on a truly deep level. I began to realize that His plan is good, that He brings the very best into our lives. His love means that His heart is filled with good will toward us and with good plans: "Thy wonderful purposes are all for our good" (Psalm 40:5, NEB).

Psalm 68:6 says that God "leads out the prisoners into prosperity" (NASB). Usually a newly released prisoner must scrounge around and start all over again from nothing (or, in fact, from less than nothing) as he tries to make something of his broken life. But when God brings us out of our spiritual and emotional prisons, He brings us forth to prosperity. He gives us a whole bank account of spiritual resources, so that we're rich.

We're not just free; we're spiritually prosperous.

Psalm 68:6 continues: "Only the rebellious dwell in a parched land." It's generally our inner rebellion—our fear of submitting to God and giving Him first place in our lives— that causes spiritual dryness and lack of satisfaction. This is not God's desire or plan for our lives. Though at times He allows dry periods to perfect our faith, His basic intention is our spiritual prosperity—life in all its fullness.

I think of Psalm 84:11 (NASB)—"No good thing does He withhold from those who walk uprightly." He won't hold back a single blessing from us if we relate to Him as Lord of our life—of our thinking and choosing, of our feelings, our actions, our relationships.

Ponder again these words in Romans 8:32 (NIV)—"He who did not spare his own Son, but gave him up for us all—how will he not also, along with him, graciously give us all things?" God gave us the very best, letting His beloved Son suffer agony so that we could belong to Him. How much more will He give us everything else that's necessary for our true joy, both in the present and throughout eternity!

If we've become God's friends by letting His Son come into our heart, will He not take care of us throughout this life and forever?

He will!

Gracious Father, You are so great and so good. I glory in the truth that You delight to do the things that delight me, that Your heart is filled with good will toward me and with good plans for me. Thank You for making me so rich in the blessings that matter most.

How I rejoice to know that You withhold no good thing from those who walk uprightly! If there are new, fresh ways You want me to walk uprightly—to let You be Lord in my life—show me. And enable me to say yes.

Give me grace to come to Your Word daily, seeking for a deeper knowledge of You as for hidden treasures. And help me count on Your love and goodness with grateful constancy.

God's words of love for me today:
Psalm 84:11-12; John 10:10; Romans 8:31-32;
2 Corinthians 8:9; 2 Peter 1:2-4

He Loves to Forgive Me

One of Satan's lies is to portray God as a severe judge who condemns His children when they sin and who is reluctant to forgive.

Satan would have us think of God responding to our sin by saying, "Won't you ever learn?" Then when we ask for forgiveness, we imagine Him saying, "Well, first I'll see how you do; I'll be glad to forgive you if you do better in the next few days. Show Me you really mean business." Satan the accuser likes to use this strategy to attack our confidence in our salvation and destroy our fellowship with the Lord. He knows this will grieve our loving Father and stunt our growth.

Of course it's true that whenever we saunter off in a

sinful direction God wants us to do an about-face, to repent. He wants us to come to Him and say, "Lord, I've been tolerating this sin, but now I turn from it and I turn back to You. I let go of it and I receive Your forgiveness. I thank You that Jesus is in me so I can have victory over this."

God loves to forgive us when we make this about-face from our sin and turn to Him. As Psalm 86:5 puts it, "You, LORD, are good, and ready to forgive" (NKJV). He welcomes us fervently just as the prodigal son's father welcomed him, leaving no room for the son to plead for his father's forgiveness (Luke 15:18-24). After we return, God wants us to simply depend on Him and on His life in us. Then we won't stray from Him as quickly or as often—though throughout our entire life we'll still need to confess one sin or another.

The story of the prodigal son is a great comfort to me. Sometimes we think it applies only to unbelievers who finally come to Christ. But I think it applies especially to the Christian life, for this runaway rascal was a *son* and had enjoyed the privileges of being in his father's family before departing for that far country.

Sometimes our own trips away are just one "little" sin, but sometimes we let many sins pile up. Eventually we realize how futile it is to go our own way, to do our own thing, as the prodigal did when he was feeding pigs and longing to fill his own stomach with the husks they were eating. We discover that sin pays poor wages.

Perhaps you've felt like telling God what the son decided to tell his father: "I am no longer worthy to be called your son." But that's as far as his father let the conversation go.

Didn't the son realize that his sonship had never been a matter of his being worthy of it? He was a son because he'd been born into the father's family. And so the father, who had been looking and longing for the opportunity to forgive and restore his son, immediately reinstated him. He wouldn't hear of his son's plan to become a hired servant and earn his way back into the family.

Nor did the father preach a sermon to his son: "Have you learned your lesson? We'll give you a little time of probation and see if you've really learned anything." No, the father ran to him, hugged and kissed him, and welcomed him right back into the love and riches of the family. There's no evidence that this father was the least bit resentful toward his son. So it is with God. Even when we're going to Him to confess sin, "we can run right into the throne room and find His arms wide open," as Kay Arthur says.

This is God's attitude when we sincerely ask His forgiveness for the things He so strongly disapproves of. He is never reluctant to forgive. He always accepts us as persons, as dearly loved children, regardless of how strongly He hates our sin—an important distinction to make.

A story from generations ago comes to mind. A young man living at home became increasingly rebellious against his parents' rules and moral standards. He just couldn't be comfortable living there. He caused quarrels and always seemed to be doing the wrong thing. Finally he decided to leave. Like the prodigal son, he traveled far from home.

At last he was able to do whatever he wanted without anyone's disapproval. This was a dream come true. But as time went by he encountered problem after problem, and his life became more and more tangled, miserable, empty. Finally he considered taking his life. But then he thought, "My only hope is to go home. I've caused my parents so much heartache, I doubt they would want me. But still…"

So he wrote a letter home. He told his parents all he had done wrong, asked them to forgive him, and expressed his desire to come home. Assuring them that he'd understand if this was not agreeable to them, he proposed the following plan. The train on which he was traveling would pass close to their house. If they were willing to have him back, would they hang a white handkerchief on the big tree in their backyard? If he saw the handkerchief as the train passed, he would get off at the next station. Otherwise he'd just keep going.

As the train rumbled toward home, he told his story to the passenger beside him. Then as they approached his parents' home, his apprehensions grew. He turned to his fellow passenger and said, "I'm afraid to look. Would you watch out the window for me?" As they finally came near, he buried his face in his hands.

Suddenly he heard the other man cry, "Look! Just look!" He raised his head and looked out. The tree in their backyard was totally covered with white handkerchiefs. There was no doubt what his parents wanted.

That's how the Lord's forgiveness is. Whether we're approaching Him for the first time to receive Him into our life or whether we're coming for the millionth time to confess a sin, He has white handkerchiefs all over the tree. He ardently welcomes us home, back into His fellowship.

I lift my heart to You, Father, rejoicing in Your loving, tender attitudes toward me day by day, hour by hour. You are so forgiving—never reluctant to forgive, always eager. It passes all human understanding how You can be so merciful and gracious to me, not giving me what I deserve and so freely giving me what I don't deserve. I praise You that I can come boldly before Your throne of grace and receive mercy for my failures and grace to help in time of need.

I praise You that through my new birth You made me completely clean, that I have been rescued, and that now I am righteous in my innermost being, fully accepted by You. Uncondemned. How good it is to trust in Your forgiveness—Your full and free forgiveness that is available every moment of every day.

Lord, cause me to stand on these truths more firmly, more constantly, and with ever-growing gratefulness.

In Jesus' name…

God's words of love for me today:
Psalms 32:4-5; 51:1-2; 66:18-20; 103:8-12;
Hosea 14:4-7; Hebrews 4:15-16

His Love
Liberates Me

I realize I'm a beginner at understanding God's love. From time to time I get my feet wet in that vast ocean of the knowledge of God. Now and then I take a plunge and swim a bit or leisurely float on my back. But all this activity is very close to shore. There's so much more, both nearby and out there beyond the mind's horizon.

Yet even as a beginner I find a delightful blend of feeling not only secure in His love, but also liberated.

Now that's a trick—to experience both security and freedom at the same time. Often they don't go hand in hand. But they come together so beautifully in our experience of God's love.

All through history, leaders of movements great and

small have promised freedom to all who would join their cause. Most of these promises have proven false. In 2 Peter 2:19 God warns us about those who lead others astray as they "promise them freedom, while they themselves are slaves of depravity—for a man is a slave to whatever has mastered him" (NIV). Most of these promises of liberty have been issued by those who were enslaved themselves. Furthermore, what they thought was liberty really wasn't.

To understand and experience God's perfect love is the only way to be truly liberated—in fact, to be more than liberated.

Jesus offers the true promise of freedom. Why did He come to this earth? In Luke 4:18 He gives His reasons: to preach good news to the poor, to proclaim release to the captives, to offer recovery of sight to the blind, and to set free the oppressed. He came to bring deliverance and sight and liberty.

And Jesus tells us in John 8:36 that if He, the Son of God, sets us free, then we are free indeed. His freedom is true freedom. And it comes through a personal relationship with Him, through His personal, loving touch on our lives as we draw near to Him.

But even as reborn children of God, when we carefully examine our lives we probably detect further areas of enslavement that we didn't know were there. We begin to see that we're in bondage to our background, to our resentment toward people, to our goals that don't line up with God's Word. We're held prisoner by attitudes we can't get rid of, by our own desires, our own emotions, and our own ways of thinking.

But the more we know God and experience His love, the more free we become. The longer we go to His Word and let His Holy Spirit teach us, the more liberation we experience. More and more our personality is freed up to become as loving and beautiful as God designed it to be.

As a picture of this freedom, Malachi 4:2 repeatedly refreshes me: "For you who fear My name, the sun of righteousness will rise with healing in its wings; and you will go forth and skip about like calves from the stall" (NASB). I especially like that final promise. Have you ever seen calves leaping about with glad abandon when released from the barn at sunrise? It's with this kind of feeling that we can celebrate our Savior's coming to earth—the long-awaited rising of the Sun of Righteousness. How we can exult that He still shines forth His healing rays to renew us spiritually and even physically!

How I thank You, Lord, for the perfect freedom You both promise and give in Your love. You are my

Liberator, my Savior. You marched into my be-
sieged life to set me free forever from sin and the
fear of death.

And You are my Lord and Master. I ask You to
show me areas of my life in which I need to turn
over the controls to You more fully. I know that the
more control I place in Your hands, the more truly
free I will become. "Make me a captive, Lord, and
then I shall be free."

Thank You that Your perfect love gives me freedom from guilt, from anxiety, from all manner of
fears. Freedom from wrong patterns of thought and
action. Freedom from excessive stress and from bur-
dens too great for me. And freedom from my in-
ability to love as You desire.

Help me day by day, hour by hour, to rise up
and soar in the freedom of Your love.

In Jesus' name…

God's words of love for me today:
Luke 4:14-19; John 8:31-36;
Hebrews 2:9,14-15; Isaiah 40:28-31; Psalm 138:3

Where My Freedom Begins

Our experience of the freedom we find in God's love begins in our mind, because our false mental notions are often at the root of our failure to trust the love of God. I like Proverbs 4:23 in the *Good News Bible:* "Be careful how you think; your life is shaped by your thoughts."

Our emotions don't just fall on us out of the blue. They generally arise from how we are thinking. Even when we're facing difficulties that trigger unusually strong and persistent emotions, we can either minimize or maximize our misery simply by the way we think. We have a choice.

We can choose to think true thoughts—thoughts that line up with reality as God has revealed it. Thoughts based on the wonderful truths God has given in His Word—

truths about Himself, about ourselves, about how life runs well, and about victory over sin and Satan.

Focusing on the *positive* realities that flood the pages of Scripture is especially important. Philippians 4:8 says that whatever is true, noble, right, pure, admirable, and worthy of praise, let your mind "dwell on these things" (NASB). This keeps us from the kind of thinking that ensnares and binds us. It prevents us from focusing on things that may not be true, things that are disreputable, wrong, impure, repulsive, and worthy of criticism or accusation.

I've often been drawn to Psalm 103:1-5. David begins the passage by tuning his heart to sing God's praise: "Bless the LORD, O my soul; and all that is within me, bless his holy name" (RSV). I'm to let my whole inner being get involved in praising Him. First, I can focus my will and my mind on God and His truth; I can choose to fix my thoughts on the Lord, on His words, and on His promises. Then I can let my emotions be touched through a steady stream of positive Philippians 4:8 thoughts—or through a calm inflow and review of a single thought, with pauses to quietly absorb the reality of who God is: "Be still, and know that I am God" (Psalm 46:10).

David continues in Psalm 103:2, "and forget none of His benefits" (NASB). The list of benefits he then gives should surely touch us emotionally and prompt enthusiastic gratitude.

He forgives all my iniquities. I am totally forgiven. I'm right in God's sight now and forever, through Christ's sacrifice! Not one smudge of guilt remains.

He heals all my diseases. By His Spirit, God brings health and strength and vitality to my whole being (Romans 8:11, Phillips).

He rescues me from the destructive pit—be it mental or emotional, physical or spiritual. "He drew me up from the desolate pit, out of the miry bog" (Psalm 40:2, RSV).

He crowns me with lovingkindness and tender mercies—or as one version says, "encompasses me." I'm surrounded and overshadowed by His mighty love.

He satisfies my desire with good things. This renews my youth. It makes me young again, restoring my strength so that I can overcome, mounting up and soaring like an eagle, as Isaiah 40:31 puts it.

These truths show the kind of God we have. He is indeed the Source of so many tremendous benefits and the inspiration for our heartfelt praise.

Psalm 126:3 says, "The LORD has done great things for us; we are glad" (NASB). Isn't that simple and powerful? I can revel in the Lord as I recall the great things He has done for us as a family and in the lives of other people. Then I can pause quietly and let myself be glad in His Presence.

Gladness is such a refreshing emotion. That is one reason why the Lord is so refreshing, for as the *King James Version* of Psalm 45:7 tells us, our King has been anointed with the oil of gladness. There is more joy and gladness with Him than with anyone else.

Isn't it refreshing to be in the company of a glad person? A glad person can walk into a room and brighten up the whole atmosphere. And isn't it discouraging to be in the company of someone whose spirit is always low, someone who's always griping and complaining and trapped in a mind-set of gloom?

But this One whom we love is anointed above all others with a contagious joy and gladness in His countenance. He's not long-faced, moody, or glum, and He doesn't want us to be that way either.

Focusing on these truths can literally change the way we think and therefore the way we feel and live. It frees us to trust in the Lord.

Lord, I give You my mind. Show me any damaging thoughts and attitudes You want to free me from. Build into my mind the positive thoughts that reflect reality—true thoughts about who You really are and who I really am.

And I rejoice, dear Lord, in the mirror of Your love where I can see so accurately who I truly am. Thank You for the security and freedom that come through Your Word, where You reveal the real truth about me, truth that is both humbling and uplifting.

May Your truth keep me from pursuing my sense of identity and security in the wrong ways, by looking in the wrong mirrors. You know how my proud flesh wants to depend on myself and other people to meet my inner needs for a secure identity, rather than looking to You.

How grateful I am for the gladness that comes when I return to the truth about You and about me. Truly it is sunshine to my heart!

And I'm grateful for the example Your gladness is to me—Your full, contagious joy. Give me grace to share in it with You more and more, and to let it shine out to those around me.

God's words of love for me today:
Psalm 26:2-3; Proverbs 4:20-23; Romans 8:15-17;
2 Corinthians 5:17; Philippians 4:4-8

He Gives Me Significance

Ralph Spaulding Cushman's "I Want the Faith" has deeply touched my life for years. The first stanza reads,

I want the faith that envies not
The passing of the days;
That sees all times and ways
More endless than the stars;
That looks at life,
Not as a little day of heat and strife,
But one eternal revel of delight
With God, the Friend, Adventurer, and Light.

I especially like the view in those last two lines. My life, too, can be "one eternal revel of delight" as I deeply and intimately experience God as my Friend, my Adventurer, my Light. The passing of earthly days won't matter, because by faith I look forward to an eternity of unhindered delight in God.

As our Adventurer, God in love gives us exciting purposes for living, better than any we can conjure up for ourselves. In His perfect love I'm freed from purposelessness and the fear of insignificance.

This is one of the big problems of modern living: Why am I here? People look and look, but fail to find a purpose big enough to really challenge them and keep them from being disappointed and frustrated with life. They try something new that promises purpose, but then it fizzles out and they feel bored and purposeless again.

God created us first of all for a loving, intimate relationship with Him, so we'll always be empty until we find that relationship. Our chief reason for existing is to glorify God and enjoy Him forever. But we cannot find that enjoyment until we begin to know Him better and to grasp His love more fully.

A popular song decades ago was titled, "You're Nobody Till Somebody Loves You." We rise far above being "nobodies" when we experience God's love. We are *somebody* in Christ.

Once more, reflect on the wonder of His love and let the truth soak in again to your heart: *The Creator and supreme Ruler of the universe desires a loving, intimate, lifelong and eternity-long relationship with—you!*

One of my favorite Christmas songs has these lines:

Long lay the world in sin and error pining
till He appeared and the soul felt its worth.

To know that we are worth more than we can imagine to Someone we admire more than we can tell—if anything can bring the true "Christmas feeling" year round, this can.

Yet we cannot experience the unshakable sense of worth He gives if we are trying to feel worthy in ourselves, if we are trying to accumulate evidence that we are good or right or significant on the human level.

When Jesus came to earth, some people already realized their failure and unworthiness apart from Him. They were ready to receive His forgiveness and the feeling of worth His love alone could give. Others first needed to have their self-esteem and "goodness" shattered.

And the paradox of Jesus' coming is this: It revealed the vastness both of our sin and of our worth to God!

His presence, like sunshine, exposes dirt that is unnoticed in dimmer light. The closer we live to Him, the more we realize the offensiveness of sin in our flesh compared to His unblemished righteousness. Yet if we have given ourselves to Him, we are clean; we are totally acquitted and made righteous; we are of priceless value to God.

Why then do we try to cover today's evidence that we are sinners, justifying our specific sins? "I'm not as bad as *she* is." "It's just my temperament." "It runs in my family." "It's John's fault." "Besides, I'm tired." Miserable attempts, aren't they? We feel so alone in them.

The Lord isn't interested in helping us maintain a sense of worth independent of Him, and He cleanses confessed sin, not excuses. So He arranges circumstances—and even uses our failures—to break through our resistance until we honestly acknowledge our specific sin.

The moment we accept the shattering of our independent self-esteem, for the first or the thousandth time, a greater truth can take over inside—the truth that we belong to the Most High God and that He delights in us. As a father treasures his child and a bridegroom his bride, so God treasures us. He has placed us in a high, unshakable position. There He increasingly works in us both to will and to do His good pleasure. He lets us share in His exciting purposes of reaching the world for Christ, as well as building up and serving His people. He has gifted each of us to play a special role in fulfilling these purposes. Talk about significance!

All through life we need to be aware of our sin and weaknesses (to humble us) and of our significance and worth in Christ (to lift us up). To maintain this dual awareness we have God's help—through His Word and prayer, through His Spirit, and sometimes through other people.

Dear Lord, exalted high above all, I worship You as the glorious Master of all creation—and as my Master. You are the God of perfect love who has included me in Your glorious eternal purposes. Thank You, Lord, for the gift of significance—that in You I can live a life of adventure and fruitfulness. Thank You for the part I can share in Your exciting plans and purposes.

I praise You for calling me out of this fallen world to be a member of Your family, a part of Your chosen, royal, and holy people. Thank You for revealing Your plans for bringing me to glory, for transforming me into the image of Your Son Jesus. Thank You that I belong to You and to Your family forever!

Enable me to be a permanent dropout from the world's race to be important in people's eyes. I leave to You the specific ways You want to glorify Yourself through my life. May I be ready each day to have You use me—or to not be used at all. Help me focus day by day on the wonder of my significance in Your sight, as Your loved one and as Your servant.

Keep refining me as a channel of Your supernatural love, so that the flow to those around me will grow fuller and sweeter.

God's words of love for me today:
1 Peter 1:3-9; 2:9; Colossians 3:17;
Matthew 28:18-20; Psalm 90:12,14,16-17

Remember to record your answer to this question:
"What verse or phrase from these passages helps me most?"

He Satisfies
My Heart

C. S. Lewis once defined history as "the long terrible story of man trying to find happiness apart from God." For so many people, that's their personal history as well.

God tells us that apart from Him and His perfect love we cannot know true happiness.

He also tells us that when we finally discover true happiness in Him, it will continue and grow only as we cultivate a deeper relationship with Him.

And He tenderly yet firmly assures us that we'll be able to experience this happiness day by day, hour by hour, if (and only if) we learn to depend on Him more constantly.

I've found that when I don't consciously depend on the Lord and His love, it's easy to become self-protective rather than happily vulnerable and expendable. I've adapted some lines by Alexander McClaren into the following prayer of commitment—a prayer that motivates me to delight in the Lord and respond to Him more quickly in every type of circumstance, large or small. Would you like to pray these words with me?

> *O God my strength, if I fix my happiness on anything less stable than the heavens, less sufficient than You, sooner or later I will lose it. If my life entwines around any earthly prop, some time or other my prop will be plucked up, my poor vine will be torn, and its sap will bleed out of it. Therefore I choose to entwine the tendrils of my life around You.*

I like to add, "My wonderful God, help me to do this more and more."

The secret of a satisfied heart is not the pursuit of satisfaction or happiness. Satisfaction and happiness are by-products of the pursuit of God. Discovering God and His love not just in our minds but also in our actual experience—this is the basis of true joy in life. It is also the basis for true growth in Christlikeness, which, in turn, brings us still greater joy.

Repeatedly Warren and I enjoy the simple way the *New Century Version* states this truth in Psalm 16:2,5-6—"You are my Lord. Every good thing I have comes from you.... The LORD is all I need. He takes care of me. My share in life has been pleasant; my part has been beautiful."

Thank You for giving me a beautiful and pleasant share in life—abundant life, life in all its fullness! I rejoice that in Your perfect love I can live in freedom and security, significance and honor. I can live with confidence that You are at work in my life to make me more like Christ. And You will faithfully complete the work You have begun.

Our God of intensely personal, overflowing love has given us Himself as our share in life. He is the source of all good things, the all-sufficient God who satisfies us with a beautiful part in life, a pleasant share.

Do you remember what Moses prayed in Psalm 90:14? "Satisfy us in the morning with thy steadfast love, that we may rejoice and be glad all our days" (RSV). All our days, he said. In both good times and hard times, an undercurrent of rejoicing can be ours, rejoicing that arises from a heart satisfied by God's unchanging love.

How I want my heart to be more consistently capti-
vated and satisfied by You, Lord, on both my good
days and my difficult days, in moments of peace and
pleasure as well as moments of pain. I ask You to
work in my heart so that this will be so—satisfy me
early, satisfy me soon, satisfy me daily with Your
steadfast love that I may rejoice and be glad in it.

What more could we really ask of life than deep satisfaction with God and, along with that, contentment with
what life brings? The psalmist wisely instructs us, "Make the
Eternal your delight, and he will give you all your heart's desire. Leave all to him, rely on him, and he will see to it"
(Psalm 37:4-5, Moffatt).

My Lord and my God, today I affirm before You that,
by Your grace, the knowledge of You and Your love
will be my life's major pursuit. This is the purpose of
my heart, for You alone are worthy.
I exult in the knowledge that You created me to
be indwelt and controlled by You, and I thank You
for showing me that my life cannot run well any
other way. You are my Master, for my good! You want
me to obey You so that it may be well with me!

I'm amazed and thrilled that Someone as wonderful as You could want my total love. Take my love, Lord God. Do what You must to open my heart so I can constantly give You more and more of it.

You will always be the biggest factor in my world, the deepest joy of my heart. I rest in the truth that the future holds You and You hold the future.

As you delight in God and manifest His fragrant love to others, you experience now a foretaste of the joyous pleasure that will be the bread and wine of heaven, when God has gathered His entire family home.

Lord of love, I worship You as the One who is majestic and tender, the source of boundless love. I praise and adore You as the One who will never fail me or disillusion me. And so, as the years go by, my heart can keep rising up to You in adoration that is ever growing, ever more delightful.

I pray that day by day I'll discover more fully how perfect Your love is, and that hour by hour I'll rest in Your intensely personal, overflowing, never-ending love for me.

You are my first love, my best love, my perfect

love. You are my highest goal, my chief delight for time and eternity.

To You be the glory forever and ever. Amen.

God's words of love for me today:

Psalms 57:9-11; 73:25-26; 89:1-2; 92:1-4; 106:1